THE FIGURE OF ECHO

John Hollander

The Figure of Echo

A MODE OF ALLUSION IN
MILTON AND AFTER

University of California Press

Berkeley • Los Angeles • London

University of California Press
Berkeley and Los Angeles, California

University of California Press, Ltd.
London, England

© 1981 by
The Regents of the University of California

Quote on page 62 from W. S. Merwin's *House and Travellers*,
copyright 1977 by W. S. Merwin, courtesy Atheneum Publishers

First Paperback Printing 1984
ISBN 0-520-05323-0

Library of Congress Cataloging in Publication Data

Hollander, John.
      The figure of echo.

      (Quantum books)
      Includes index.
      1. Allusions in literature. 2. English poetry—
History and criticism. 3. American poetry—History
and criticism. 4. Echo in literature. I. Title.
PR508.A44H64   821'.009'15   80-26227

Printed in the United States of America

1   2   3   4   5   6   7   8   9

For Angus Fletcher

The Widener Burying-Ground

In spite of all the learned have said,
We hear the voices of the dead.
Not scholiasts who like Burke and Hare
Turn dead leaves in the living air,
Unlock the Essay and exhume
Philosophy from its dry tomb,
Nor wise embalmers of the text
In humble buckram or perplexed,
Carved, interlaced half-calf, who come
To show how gold they are, and dumb—
We strike from silent lines a fire.
Troped sea-shell, loud Aeolian liar,
Nymph-haunted cave and mountain-peak
Choir with voices that we seek
As, scholars of one candle-end,
We hear the hush of dusk descend.
We unfired vessels of the day,
Built of a soft, unechoing clay,
Grow obdurate of ear at night

When images of voice are bright:
The dreamingale, the waterlark,
Within the present, silent dark
Echo the burden (on these stairs
Mistranslated) the singer bears—
He who packs, with a glowing faith,
In one portmanteau, fame and death.
Our marginalia all insist
—Beating the page as with a fist
Against a silent headstone—that
The dead whom we are shouting at,
Though silent to us now, have spoken
Through us, their stony stillness broken
By our outcry (*We are the dead
Resounding voices in our stead*)
Until they strike in us, once more,
Whispers of their receding shore,
And Reason's self must bend the ear
To echoes and allusions here.

Contents

Preface

In these pages I consider a way of alluding that is inherently poetic, rather than expository, and that makes new metaphor rather than learned gestures. In contrasting poetic echo with modes of more overt allusion, I don't take up problems of actual or putative audience, or of the degree of self-awareness, of conscious design, in poetic response to the very words of an earlier text. I am content here to observe that poems seem to echo prior ones for the personal aural benefit of the poet, and of whichever poetic followers can overhear the reverberations. Poets also seem to echo earlier voices with full or suppressed consciousness that, and of how, they are doing so, by accident or by plan, but with the same shaping spirit that gives form to tropes of thought and feeling. Whether these figurative echoes constitute a kind of underground cipher-message for the attentive poetic ear, or perhaps a private melody or undersong hummed during composition by the poet as a spell or charm, matters less to me than that the revisionary power of allusive echo generates new figuration. Theories of consciousness, intention, and the hermeneutics of overhearing may attempt answers to these and other questions that it has been my pleasure and concern to raise.

I have not attempted anything like a systematic taxonomy of allusive echoic patterns. Neither have I outlined a thematic investigation of, say, the Miltonic echoes in *The Prelude*. Tasks like these would extend far beyond this volume's quantum of scope. I have, however, added an appendix on the nature and history of the trope of transumption.

Although some readers may feel that it overloads what is an intuitive and personal essay, it seemed to me essential to be able to call the operation of intertextual echo by its proper name, especially since that name is shared by a large family of revisionary poetic elements. Those readers who are content to treat *transumption* as a coinage can dispense with the account of the term's history, which, as far as I know, has not hitherto been recorded.

It will be clear that I am primarily interested in poetry in English. My concern for origins—both mythological and formal—of "echo" used figuratively rather than literally calls for a consideration of a few classical texts. But I have not touched upon echoes within Greek and Latin poetry, having neither the knowledge nor the intuitive authority; a reader interested in pursuing such questions further might start with Gordon Williams' splendid *Tradition and Originality in Roman Poetry*.

I am most grateful to Harold Bloom, Richard Poirier, Heinrich von Staden, and Arnold Stein, who read all or part of this study in earlier stages and made valuable suggestions. David Bromwich, Nicholas Howe, Carmela Perri, George Pigman, Edwin Stein, and Edward Tayler were extremely helpful; directing Joseph Loewenstein's dissertation, in which he pursued Echo's mythography much further than I have, was most instructive. Work on this book proceeded with help from the A. Whitney Griswold Research Fund at Yale and, in its later stages, from the John Simon Guggenheim Memorial Foundation. My final debts are two: to the dedicatee of this volume, whose very asides and footnotes have been, for a generation of interpreters, oracular; and to Natalie Charkow, for encouragement and admonition, each when I had no need of the other.

I.
Echo Acoustical

Echoes are the reflections of sounds from solid surfaces. They are distinguished, in acoustical terminology, from reverberations generally in reaching the listening ear at least one-fifteenth of a second after the originating sound. Reverberations attending more closely upon the source affect us not as repetitions, but rather by prolonging the originating sound or altering its apparent timbre. As in the case of mirrored light, the angle of incidence of sound waves is equal to the angle of reflection, and convex surfaces will converge echoes so as to make them louder and more noticeable than rebounds from planar surfaces. An echo of any given delay—say of a full second (from a distance of about 543 feet)—will only clearly return sound of that duration or less; the primary sound of a longer phrase of speech or music will interfere with the sound of the echo, and only the last second's worth of the phrase will be heard unconfused with its source. It is for this reason that echoes seem to return fragments of speech. Complex conformations of reflecting surfaces—in rocks, caves, forests, and spacious, intricate interiors of stone and masonry—can produce serial echoes—echoes themselves reechoed—as well as divers direct reflections from various distances. These are appreciably fainter than the first of the series.

Mountains provide sufficiently distant reflecting surfaces, and caves sufficiently varied concave ones, so that echoes seem, as disembodied voices, to inhabit such regions. Until an astoundingly late moment in the history of technology—that of Edison's sound transcription—the only means of perpetuating sound per se (as opposed to writing and musical notation, which preserve instructions for producing it) were echoes, and perhaps parrots (save for the charming fable of frozen echoes, or the voices of mariners flung up from shipboard in wintry northern seas, and released again in summer thawing). Echoing was understood as reflection in classical times, even by thinkers who, like Democritus, the author of the Aristotelian *Problemata,* Lucretius, and Seneca, among others, believed that sounds were transmitted as discrete entities imprinted on the air. One theorist could hold that echoes were reflected better by dry walls (in caves, etc.—thus *Problemata* XI, 7), and Francis Bacon, in projecting an experiment "concerning the super-reflexion of echoes" (*Silva silvarum,* Cent. VIII, 795) could note that "all echoes sound better against old walls than new; because they are more dry and hollow." In both cases, some trace of mythology clings to the reasoning, suggesting a more privileged milieu independent of acoustic fact (Bacon's older walls might be more reflective because of the materials of their surfaces; the hollowness would be acoustically irrelevant, but suggests caves). This association of concavity with a lurking and invisible vocal presence is central to what the imagination has made of the phenomenon of echo.

The history of scientific acoustics remained much closer to the phenomenology of perceived sound, up to the eighteenth century, than did that of optics or mechanics to the apparent facts of vision and motion. Resonance, or the creation of large vibrations in a sounding body by smaller ones in phase with them, is a concept whose grasp depended upon sophisticated mathematical developments for the analysis of harmonic vibrations. The seventeenth-century Franciscan encyclopedist of music and sound, Marin Mersenne, was fascinated by echoes and employed them in experiments intended to calibrate the velocity of sound in air.

He wrote on the reflective properties of the various conic sections and even fancied a projected discipline of "Echometry," which might cope with such intriguing problems as (1) echoes that could respond up to twenty times, with the final repetition louder than the initial ones; (2) portable echo chambers, like portable mirrors; (3) echoes that would answer in Spanish what was cried out in French; (4) echoes that would respond to a tone at the octave or fifth; (5) echoes that would store the sound and reflect only at certain times of day or night; and so forth.[1]

Mythologies of echo have depended variously upon the phenomenology of reflected sound. In modern discourse, the word *echo* is used figuratively to indicate a musical or linguistic repetition, usually of a short utterance or the terminal portion of a longer one, with the additional qualification that the repeated sound is not only contingent upon the first, but in some way a qualified version of it (a metaphor of the decaying dynamics of successive echoes, perhaps). In the following pages, certain aspects of this figure of echo are examined in the light of their significance for poetry. The echoing discussed will not be literal; the terms *echo, reverberation,* and *resonance* will be used figuratively and often synonymously, without regard to their technical meanings. And yet the acoustic phenomena of echo—caves and mountains and halls of origin, delays in return, scattering and proliferation, and so forth—will be implicitly and explicitly invoked, as will certain conceptual problems arising from them. Alexander Bryan Johnson, the nineteenth-century

1. Figurative versions of (1) through (5) do exist; it is the view of the last three chapters of this book that they are poems. For more on echometry, see Athanasius Kircher's encyclopedic *Musurgia universalis* IX, I. His physical version of an echo text of the sort dealt with in chapter 3, below, is to be seen in the illustration in chapter 1—an artificial echo which has walls so placed that the shouted word *clamore* ("O outcry") becomes reechoed as the Italian words for "love," "delays," "hours," and, finally, "king."

Artificial schematic echo. See chapter 1, note 1. This woodcut may also be taken as a mechanical model of the rhetorical effect studied in chapter 3. From Athanasius Kircher, *Neue Hall -und Thonkunst* (Nördlingen, 1684), the Beinecke Rare Book and Manuscript Library, Yale University.

philosopher of language, felt that if we ask whether the sound is part of the thunder, "the question only embarrasses." The idolatry, and the joyful conceptual messiness, of trope and all its works are beyond that embarrassment; and such matters as the inherence of voice in source, and the relative presences of either, will arise in shadow and in substance in the following pages. The question whether unmarked whiteness, or blackness, is a more appropriate trope of silence will, however, not be considered.

II.
Echo Allegorical

Echo enters our poetry long before Ovid's famous nymph. Any mythology of echoing must deal with such aspects of the acoustical phenomenon as the fragmentary repetition, the decrescendo, and the presence of disembodied voice. We first hear echoes in Homer as reverberations and amplifications of battle noise or of trees falling in forests. They can be fearful, as when the rocks roar around the shouting Polyphemus (*Odyssey* IX, 395). In Hesiod, however, echoing sounds begin to take on some of the significances they possess in later poetry.

When the Muses sing at the beginning of the *Theogony* "all the mansion of Zeus the father / of the deep thunder is joyful in the light voice of the goddesses / that scatters through it, and the peaks of snowy Olympus re-echo [*echei*]" (lines 40–42, in Richmond Lattimore's translation), the contrast between the heavy, loud sound *(erigdoupoio)* of Zeus and the lilylike *(leirioesse),* scattered voices of the goddesses concentrates on the delight engendered by the latter in the realm of the former.[1] The reverberations of white-lilied singing appropriately come from snow-white peaks, although no specific allegory of confirmation or approving applause is manifest here.

Twenty-odd lines further on, however, the Muses ascend to Olympus (again, in Lattimore's version) "in immortal music, and all the black earth re-echoed *(iache)* to them / as they sang, and the lovely beat of their footsteps sprang beneath them / as they hastened to their father" (lines 69–71).

---

1. Hesiod, *Theogony,* trans. Richmond Lattimore (Ann Arbor, 1959), 125.

Here the response of the dark and heavy to what is in both senses light—of resonance to dancing—is much closer to that later pastoral echoing which from Theocritus and Virgil on comes to be associated with a response of nature, in kind, to poetic discourse itself. Inasmuch as Hesiod is trying to authenticate his own poem by praising the Muses at such length, the echoing in the text here affirms the poem's own immortality.

But we notice that although these are Olympian, or mountain, echoes, they are embodied in no Oreads or mountain nymphs who sing them back. The personifications of Echo herself come later in literary tradition, Even before Ovid's central and canonical association of reverberating sound with reflected light in *Metamorphoses* III—we shall come to it shortly—we have the association of the nymph Echo with Pan. In the Homeric Hymn to Pan (admittedly late) we have a description of the god's evening music, his unsurpassed piping, and "Then do the nymphs of the mountain accompany Pan with soprano / Voices, and, nimble of foot, by the side of a spring of dark water / Wander and chant, meanwhile Echo makes moan round the tops of the mountains" (XIX, 19–21, trans. Daryl Hine).[2] Here we are closer to the Virgilian realm.

Pan's love of Echo, and his fathering of her daughter Irynx—whether she was Oread or Dryad—is at the heart of one tradition of fable about her. The specific problem of an echo's fragmentation of speech is nicely handled in the version of Echo which Daphnis expounds to Chloe in Longus' third-century romance: Echo was a wood-nymph, but mortal; taught by the Muses to sing and play all the wind and string instruments, she

danced with the Nymphs and sung in consort with the Muses, but fled from all males, whether men or Gods, because she loved vir-

2. *The Homeric Hymns,* trans. Daryl Hine (New York, 1972), 69.

ginity. Pan sees that, and takes occasion to be angry at the maid,
and to envy her music because he could not come at her beauty.
Therefore he sends a madness among the shepherds . . . and they
tore her all to pieces and flung about them all over the earth her yet
singing limbs [*adonta ta melê,* punning on limbs and songs]. The
Earth in observance of the Nymphs buried them all, preserving to
them still their music property, and they by an everlasting sentence
and decree of the Muses breathe out a voice. And they imitate all
things now as the maid did before, the Gods, men, organs [instru-
ments], beasts. Pan himself they imitate too when he plays on the
pipe; which when he hears he bounces out and begins to post over
the mountains, not so much as to catch and hold as to know what
clandestine imitator that is that he has got.

This account, which I quote in George Thornley's Elizabethan version, is the one which Daphnis gives Chloe, after
her first experience of an acoustical echo, and in exchange
for ten kisses. Clearly, some of the details are appropriate to
the narrative occasion. But the story of the fragmentation is
potent enough, and the preservation of song in broken
pieces is central to this myth of musical echo.

The Ovidian story, however, concerns language. In *Metamorphoses* III (356–510), the nymph was originally a mere
chatterbox, cleverly holding Juno's attention (*longo prudens
sermone tenebat*) while the rest of her nymphs ran off to
Jupiter. Juno discovering this, she reduced Echo into what
we should call today a voice-activated device, unable to
originate discourse, unable to forbear from reply. In the
association of Echo with Narcissus, the profoundest relations between light and sound, emptiness and fullness of
self, absorption and reflection, are established. Ovid's story
of Echo's hopeless love for the autoleptic youth follows the
spurned nymph into the woods and, finally, into what will
be thenceforth her canonical domain, rocky caves (*solis ex
illo vivit in antris*). Within such hollow spaces she withers
away into a voice speaking out of bones; then the bones

petrify in time, and the voice speaking out of woodland
caves—for Ovid transports her from the mountainous and
Olympian realm of the Oread to the Dryadic one—will
forever remain voice only, unseen, but ever heard.

From the fables of Pan and Narcissus, two strands of
mythographic interpretation descend from medieval to late
Renaissance interpreters. A little epigram of Ausonius (ca.
A.D. 3), frequently quoted by later commentators, identifies
Echo as the daughter of air and language (*aeris et linguae sum
filia*); in George Sandys' seventeenth-century translation:

> Fond Painter, why wouldst thou my picture draw?
> An unknowne Goddesse, whom none ever saw.
> Daughter of aire and tongue: of judgment blind
> The mother I; a voice without a mind.
> I only with anothers language sport:
> And but the last of dying speech retort.
> Lowd Ecchos mansion in the eare is found:
> If therefore thou wilt paint me, paint a sound.
>
> (Vane, quid adfectas faciem mihi ponere, pictor,
>   ignotamque oculis sollicitare deam?
> Aeris et Linguae sum filia, mater inanis
>   indicii, vocem quae sine mente gero.
> extremos pereunte modos a fine reducens,
>   ludificata sequor verba aliena meis.
> auribus in vestris habito penetrabilis Echo:
>   et, si vis similem pingere, pinge sonum.)

In fact, mythographers would be painting more than
sound. Macrobius allegorizes Echo as celestial harmony,
married to Pan who, as creator of the sevenfold pipe, is also
thereby creator of the sevenfold planetary music; she is invisible to human sight, and an apt symbol of the *harmonia
coeliae* which cannot be perceived by our senses (*Saturnalia*
I, 22). There is a tendency in this tradition of interpretation
to pair or closely associate Echo and Syrinx: certainly Pan's

sigh of disappointment at the armful of reeds he came up
with when he clutched for the metamorphosed nymph,
blowing through those very reeds and producing *sonum
tenuem similemque querenti*—"a faint and plaintive sound"—
as Ovid puts it (*Metamorphoses* I, 708), is a version of an
echo. Later commentators continue this positive or aug-
mentative reading of Echo: Boccaccio, Giraldi, Cartari,
Conti, and others all affirm it and usually continue on to a
discussion of Syrinx as well. Some demythologize as is their
wont—thus Alexander Ross (in *Mystagogus poeticus,* 164):
"His falling in love with *Echo* was to shew how shepherds
who lived in woods and caves (where the greatest *Ecchos* are
most commonly) took delight to hear the resoundings of
their music." Some, like Francis Bacon, expand brilliantly
and elaborately the signification of the relation of Pan or the
natural world with a voice:

For the world enjoys itself, and in itself all things that are. . . . The
world itself can have no loves or any want (being content with
itself) unless it be of *discourse.* Such is the nymph Echo, a thing not
substantial but only a voice; or if it be more of the exact and
delicate kind, *Syringa,*—when the words and voices are regulated
and modulated by numbers, whether poetical or oratorical. But it
is well devised that of all words and voices Echo alone should be
chosen for the world's wife, for that is the true philosophy which
echoes most faithfully the voices of the world itself, and is written
as it were at the world's own dictation, being nothing else than the
image and reflection thereof, to which it adds nothing of its own,
but only iterates and gives it back.
  (*De dignitate et augmentis scientarum,* II, xiii, trans. Ellis and Spedding)

This marriage is one of nature to the true poetry of natural
philosophy, the marriage for which he himself claims, in the
Novum organum, to be writing the spousal verse or epithala-
mium. Even Marin Mersenne, hardly as much a poet as
Bacon is, in the middle of his simple but detailed mathemat-

ical discussion of the propagation of echoes in the first book of his *Harmonie universelle* (1636) himself sighs regretfully that he leaves many problems for "un autre Pan, c'est à dire un homme plus universel, que je ne suis en toute sorte d'autres cognoissances pour attraper cette fuyarde" (I, 51).

In general, it is in the milieu of Pan that Echo becomes a credential voice, associated with truth rather than with the qualities of the other Echo, the spurned lover of the self-loving Narcissus.[3] The mythographic commentators on Ovid are fairly unambiguous. Echo is a boaster ("Echo allegorice significat iactantium") in Georg Sabinus' *Metamorphosis seu fabulae poeticae* (Frankfurt, 1589), and her love for Narcissus is the boasting of self-love; she is a flatterer for Pierre Bersuire in his commentary on Ovid (Lyon, 1518), and for Bacon in *De sapienta veterum.* The negative readings of Echo come from associations of fragmentation of the anterior voice, the hollowness of her concavities of origin transferred to the figurative hollowness of her words, and the progressive diminution of successive reverberations. George Sandys adds to his translation of Ausonius in his lengthy commentary on Ovid's story that "the image of voice[4] so often rendered, is as that of the face reflected from one glasse to another; melting by degrees, and every reflection more weak and shady than the former." Echo is

3. Professor Gloria Kury's forthcoming study of Luca Signorelli's lost painting of Pan will cast some new light on the poetic mythography of Echo in the Renaissance, particularly with respect to the relation between the two nude figures in the painting. See also Poussin's *Birth of Bacchus,* which may contain an implicit comment on Echo's association with both Pan and Narcissus.

4. This phrase, whether used by Sandys or much later on by Wordsworth in "The Power of Sound," comes from the fairly literal Latin use of *imago,* or sometimes *imago vocis,* for *echo.* It precedes, rather than tropes, our primarily visual use of the word *image.* Thus Horace, *Carmina* I. 12. 4–5 "cuius recinet iocosa/nomen imago," where the applauding mountaintops hark back to Hesiod as well as to Pindar. Likewise, Horace I, 20; Virgil *Georgics* IV, 50, and elsewhere.

nevertheless a powerful mocker, and as we shall see shortly, Ovid's poetic device in telling her story becomes in later poetry a way of deconstructing words, often of love, into their hidden but operative *ultimae* (thus Du Bellay: "Qu'est-ce qu'aimer et se plaindre souvent?"—"Vent," Echo answers). If Pan's echo is lyric, Narcissus' is satiric.

Other moralizing traditions develop from the older poetic use of echo in a less strongly personified way. The echo that is fame or applause—so Horace in the *Odes* I, 12 and I, 20—shows up in the medieval *Ovide moralisé* as *bone renomée,* outlasting Narcissus' beauty, existing only in the voices of others, and as *bona fama* in Arnolphe d'Orleans; *resonare* when applied to a name means renown.

A purely acoustical treatment of the phenomenon of echo, the one by Lucretius (*De rerum natura* IV, 570–93), can hover at the brink of interpretation. In speaking of sounds which can delude us with *imagine verbi* or echoes, he remarks how in lonely places (*loca sola*) the very rocks return our utterances when we search for straying companions and call out after them. The philosopher's example unwittingly becomes an important element of fable; as we shall see, the role of questioning is crucial in the literary device of the echo song or text. Woods or rocks, empty of human presence, become the scene of inquiry—from "Where are you hiding?" to "Echo, where are *you* hiding?" is a short step. A cave hides both body and disembodied voice.

Lucretius' commentary is notable for the powerful demystifying at the end of it. After beautifully rendering the effect of a six- or sevenfold echo he had himself heard—"so did hills themselves to hills push back the words and repeat the echo" ("ita colles collibus ipsi / verba repulsantes iterabant dicta referri")—he turns aside. Echoes such as these, he continues, cause imagined nymphs and satyrs to come into being, as well as fables of Pan himself, the fanciers of such fables not wishing to be thought to inhabit a place deserted

even by the gods. The literary milieu is that of pastoral
questing and lament for loss: whether in Bion or Moschus;
or in Virgil's reference in his sixth *Eclogue* to the legendary
search by the Argonauts for Hylas, until the whole shore
rang "Hylas! Hylas!" ("ut litus Hyla, Hyla omne sonaret");
or even the allusive *vocis imago* of this same line in Valerius
Flaccus' *Argonautica* (III, 596–97), "Again 'Hylas' and again
'Hylas' he calls through the empty distances," the forest
caves responding accordingly ("rursus Hylan et rursus Hylan per longa reclamat / avia"). The hue and cry for the loss
of a friend or lover is echoed by the emptiness he or she
leaves. We are led back to the realm of Pan, but by a different
way, through a region in which echo is not personified, but
instead remains a dominant trope of acoustical vocal
image.[5]

5. The mythography of Echo is vast; I have attempted here to do no more
than distinguish the two patterns of association with Pan and Narcissus.
Interested readers may pursue this further by considering Pindar, *Olympian* 14, where Echo brings a bright message to the dark wall of the un-
derworld (as opposed to the parallel moment in *Olympian* 8, where the
same task is given to *Angelia*). Lucian, *On the Gods* and *The Double Indict-
ment* take up matters of mockery and strife between Pan and Echo; likewise, Nonnos, *Dionysiaca,* XV, 388; XVI 288, etc., and Philostratus,
Eikones II, 11, where Echo scorns Pan. The later group of *ekphrases* by
Callistratus relate the myths of Echo and the statue of Memnon (nos. 1 and
9); that stone image was given voice by the light of its mother, Dawn,
falling upon it, and thereby parallels Echo, whose body became stone. (For
E. A. Poe, in "The Coliseum," these are both associated with the voices of
ruins: " 'Not all'—the Echoes answer me—'not all / 'Prophetic sounds and
loud, arose forever / 'From us, and from all Ruin, unto the wise, / 'As
melody from Memnon to the sun.' ") There are interesting acoustical discussions in Pliny XXXVI, 22; Varro, *Res rusticae* III. 16. 12, and in Servius
and other commentators on Virgil (on *Eclogues* I and VI and *Georgics* IV.
See also Persius, *Prologue,* 11; and I, 102. In Lactantius, *Narratio fabularum*
III, 5 and *Mythologicum vaticanum* II, 180, Echo hides in caves because of her
ugliness. Then there are Boccaccio, *Genealogia deorum gentilium* I, 59; Lilio
Gregorio Giraldi, *De deii gentium* V, 138–39; Vincenzo Cartari, *Le
imagini. . .degli Dei* on Pan and Echo, likewise Richard Lynche, *The Foun-
taine of Ancient Fiction;* Stephanus' *Dictionarium historicum, geographicum,*

For Echo's pastoral identity is another matter. There are hints that echoing constitutes applause or affirmation or sympathetic resonance in Hesiod and the Homerica. Theocritus' shepherd Thyrsis speaks of the sweet music of the whispering pine tree beside a spring as comparing with the sweet melody of the goatherd's pipe; the latter, in turn, praises Thyrsis' music for having the same sweetness of sound as a gentle waterfall (*Idyll* I, 1–3, 78). These antiphonal sounds are not strictly echoes. But there is a kind of mutual confirmation of the various noises, human and natural, in the pastoral *locus amoenus*. In Virgil's first eclogue, the shepherd Tityrus is moved by his *otium*—"lentus in umbra / formosam resonare doces Amaryllida silvas"—at ease in the shade to teach the woods to echo the name of fair Amaryllis: his poems would do the teaching, and, by implication, the woods would authenticate the poetic sound in the tones of Theocritan approval. The name *Amaryllis* itself, associated by some Renaissance commentators with splendor or shining (as if from *amarugê,* or "twinkling") plays a part in a most definitely un-Ovidian relation of light and shade to sound and silence. Generally, the pastoral echo is a version of the Olympian sounds of confirmation, taken down

---

poeticum. The Echo of Nicholas Renouard's *Les metamorphosis d'Ovide* (1618) remains responsive to the "piteous accents of lovers as desolate as herself," while that of Abraham Fraunce's *The Third Part of the Countess of Pembroke's Yvychurch* (1592) is truly "Junoes daughter, for she is nothing else but the reverberation and reduplication of the ayre." Also, "T. H.," *The Fable of Ovid Treating of Narcissus* (1560); Alexander Neckham, *De naturis rerum,* etc.; William Warner, *Albion's England;* Blaise de Vigenère's translation of Philostratus, *Les Images* (1614); Michel de Marolles, *Tableaux du temple des Muses* (1655), which gives many classical and modern sources; and Thomas Blackwell, *Letters Concerning Mythology* (1748), Letter VIII. Poussin may have consulted François Habert, *Histoire du beau Narcisse* (1550). In Petrarch's canzona (*Rime* 23), Echo is associated with both Actaeon and Narcissus.

from the rocky heights, but not, as in Ovid, for a satiric reduction.

Pastoral echoing, which Thomas Rosenmeyer has so eloquently explored,[6] is an important motif throughout Virgil's eclogues. In the final one we have a recapitulation of the opening, but with a wider significance for a widened poetic genre: "non canimus surdis, respondent omnia silvae"—"we sing not to the deaf, all the forests respond." The woods and hills of the pastoral fiction continue to do so for centuries. The refrain of Spenser's "Epithalamion" (at its canonical, first statement) renders the figurative significance of what we shall consider shortly as the Echo scheme in its very verse structure. The English alexandrine, with its tendency to fracture into trimeter half-lines, a pattern that is rhetorically one of formal scheme, is put to deeper figurative purposes. "The woods shall to me answer and their echo ring" has the metaphoric "answer" of the woods—an interpretive summation of the Virgilian—itself followed by the mere literal "and their echo ring." (The whole effect is underlined by the inversion of "to me answer." "Answer to me" might be rhythmically as effective, but would prevent the closely following, quasi-echoic assonance of "*an*swer *an*d.")[7] But this is a new and complex literalism, rather than merely a shedding of figuration, and presupposes the affirmative role of the pastoral echo.

One minor but important tradition gives echo a divine or prophetic character. The Neoplatonist mythographer Henry Reynolds appends to his remarkable little treatise *Mythomystes* (1632) the tale of Narcissus in *ottava rima*,

6. Thomas G. Rosenmeyer, *The Green Cabinet* (Berkeley, Los Angeles, and London, 1969), 148–50, 185–86.
7. In *The Faerie Queene* VI. xxvi 6, when Calidore finds the pastoral green world destroyed, even echo is emptied: "The woods did nought but ecchoes vaine rebound."

"briefly Mythologised" in a prose commentary. After running through a number of readings, including a moral one—*"Ecco,* or Fame (a faire voice) loves and wooes *Narcissus,* or *Philautia"* who "despises and slights the more to be imbraced happinesse of a lasting renowne, and memory"— Reynolds moves to "a much higher and nobler meaning then any of these before delivered." Citing Iamblichus, Reynolds reports that Pythagoras propounded his ideas in "figurative, tipick and symbolick Notions; among which, one of his documents is this—*While the winds breathe, adore Ecco."* And he continues:

This *Winde* is (as the before-mentioned Iamblicus, by consent of his other fellow-*Cabalists* sayes) the Symbole of the Breath of God; and Ecco, the Reflection of this divine breath, or Spirit upon us; or (as they interpret it) *the daughter of the divine voice*; which through the beatifying splendor it shedds and diffuses through the Soule, is justly worthy to be reverenced and adored by us. This *Ecco* descending upon a Narcissus, or such a Soule as (impurely and vitiously affected) slights, and stops his eares to the Divine voice, or shutts his harte from divine Inspirations, through his being enamour'd of not himselfe, but his owne shadow meerely . . . he becomes thence . . . an earthy, weake, worthlesse thing, and fit sacrifize for only eternall oblivion. . . .

"Daughter of a divine voice" is obviously the rabbinic *bat kol,* "daughter of a voice" as it was usually explained, a phrase which means "echo" in modern Hebrew, and which referred to a secondary, or derivative, voice of the holy spirit. Often uttering a scriptural text, such a voice, as it were an echo of heaven, seems to have had at best a contingent authority.[8] Thus Milton (*Paradise Lost* IX, 653–54): "God so commanded, and left that Command / Sole Daughter of his voice," and, following him, Wordsworth's

8. See the discussion in Max Kadushin, *The Rabbinic Mind* (New York, 1952), 261–63, and the entry in the *Encyclopedia Judaica* on *bat kol.*

Duty, "stern Daughter of the Voice of God."

Reynolds' association of the *bat kol* in this version with Narcissus' nymph moves silently through an association with Pan's consort as well. This is a kind of echo transcendent, and appears in later poetry in the tropes by which the natural phenomena of echo are handled. Reynolds may indeed have had his own "tipick and symbolick" notion here in a private allegory about the nature of poetry itself; Echo would thus constitute the major mythopoetic tradition in whose behalf the polemic in *Mythomystes* is directed. Traces of this association with poetic truth are discernible in the delicate revision of the Ovidian fable in Ben Jonson's *Cynthia's Revels*. Echo, had not Narcissus spurned her, "would have dropt away her selfe in teares, / Till shee had turn'd all water, that in her, / (As in a truer glasse) thou might's have gazed" (*Cynthia's Revels* I, ii). The figurative mirror of language, of text, would have allowed the youth to perceive his beauty "by more kind reflection" than mere visual image could provide.

Echo's heavenly role is subtly underlined in Milton's revisions of the last two lines of the Lady's song to Echo in *Comus*. The presence invoked by the lost girl is a remarkable composite of the figures of echo associated with Narcissus and with Pan; Milton's "Sweet Queen of Parley, Daughter of the Sphere" is hardly the *babillarde* of many moralizers, but the regent of discourse. If she can indeed tell the Lady where her lost brothers are, she will thereby be fully elevated into the highest realm of transfiguration: "So mayst thou be transplanted to the skies, / And hold a counterpoint to all Heav'n's Harmonies." In revising the text of the masque for publication under his own name, Milton reworked these lines to preserve the musical image which emphasized the final transformation of echo into *harmonia coeli,* but with yet more resonance: "So mayst thou be translated. . . . / And give resounding grace." "Translated" is particularly important here, for its meanings range from metamorphosis through its modern linguistic application; the nymph will be translated, the word *echo* will be translated, into a higher realm of both music and language, and to the sound of a sort of solemn music.

From the mid-seventeenth century on, the acoustical phenomenon itself, with or without the decorative application of the moralized nymph, inhabits a realm of figurative language as dense as any literal woods.[9] Abraham Cowley (in "Eccho" from *The Mistresse,* 1647) expands in a conceited vein upon sonic rebound: "Shapes by reflexion shapes beget: / The voice it selfe, when stopt, does back retire, / And a new voice is made by it. / Thus things by opposition / The gainers grow. . . ." Henry Vaughan's beautiful Latin "Ad Echum" (from *Olor Iscanus,* 1651), prays for guidance through the secrets and intricacies of virgin forest. Alexander Pope's "the sound must seem an echo to the sense" takes the hedged risk of simile only in translating echo to the linguistic realm. In later poetry natural echoes remain relatively hollow or resonant, along a spectrum parallel to that lying between the nymphs of Narcissus and Pan (thus, for example, G. M. Hopkins' leaden echo—repeating "Despair"—and golden one—reiterating "Yonder"—from *St. Winefred's Well*).

The subsequent history of echo allegorical is too complex to be traced here. I shall only indicate an important direction taken by romantic images of echoing which trope the phenomenon and the older mythology, but without direct appeal even to traces of the latter. Echoing, for Wordsworth, is so central a figure of representation and plays such an im-

9. By 1657, the poetic cliches about echo listed in Joshua Poole's *The English Parnassus* have "pratling, twatling, babling, tearing, loud, resounding, shrill, vocal, heavy, cavy, talking, solitary, wood-haunting, wandering, roving, piercing" as epithets. See also Poole's amusing cento from published poems.

portant part in the dialogue of nature and consciousness that
it would require an extensive separate treatment.

In an interesting later poem, "The Power of Sound," he
seems almost to sum up the mythological history of echo:

> Ye Voices, and ye Shadows
> And Images of voice—to hound and horn
> From rocky steep and rock-bestudded meadows
> Flung back, and in the sky's blue cave reborn—
> On with your pastime! till the church-tower bells
> A greeting give of measured glee;
> And milder echoes from their cells
> Repeat the bridal symphony.

The traditional Latin *imago* here becomes a complex figure,
blending a far more visual meaning of *image* (appositive to
"shadow") with something approaching our modern sense
of *image* meaning "trope." It is the metaphor of echoing
which is reborn in the "sky's blue cave"; that cave is itself a
rebirth of Echo's "airy Shell" in *Comus* even as Milton had
opened out the echo-haunted forest caves into the openness,
rather than the hollowness, of the cosmos.

So, too, with the highly charged echoes in *The Prelude*
(the skating episode and stealing the boat in Book I) and,
more remarkably, the "echoes loud, / Redoubled and redoubled" returned to the Boy of Winander. These all move
us into extremely complex relationships of light and sound,
and of the originality of repetition, far beyond the imaginative consequences of the traditional mythology. Wordsworth's metamorphosed echoing itself enters the history
of mythology. A later poet, Robert Frost, full of a sense of
the irrecoverable force of the earlier voice, tried to ring
from the echoing landscape of poetry not "the mocking
echo of his own" cry across a lake, not life's "own love back
in copy speech," "but counter-love, original response."
Frost's framing of echoes of origination in "The Most of It"

produces not a nymph, but a mythologically ambiguous buck unspeaking save in sounds of forest and water.

However, the originality of Frost's response recalls Thoreau's reinvestiture of Echo as the consort of Pan, in the wonderful "Sounds" chapter of *Walden,* where he hears the sounds of distant church bells,

> a melody which the air had strained, and which had conversed with every leaf and needle of the wood, that portion of the sound which the elements had taken up and modulated and echoed from vale to vale. The echo is, to some extent, an original sound, and therein is the magic and charm of it. It is not merely a repetition of what was worth repeating in the bell, but partly the voice of the wood; the same trivial words and notes sung by a wood-nymph. [10]

The nymph returns for Thoreau, even as an appositive figure of speech. Yet for other romantic images of echo, even the babbling, chiding nymph of Narcissus can become strangely beneficent: Kierkegaard, who elsewhere uses the phrase "as malicious as Echo's heartless mockeries," can turn this about—"I have but one friend, Echo; and why is Echo my friend? Because I love my sorrow, and Echo does not take it away from me" (*Diapsalmata ad te ipsum*). [11] But here the speaker is himself a version of Narcissus. More complex and insidious is Nietzsche's echo, which, as a trope of the trope that purports to be literal, is an epistemological mocker and deceiver: Nietzsche characterizes the literalist, the scientist, as a seeker who without knowing it "contemplates the whole world as related to man, as the infinitely protracted echo of an original sound: man; as the multiplied copy of one arch-type: man." Echo is here the metaphor that

10. George Meredith's lines on the sound of trees being hacked down in the woods recast the nymph and the acoustic effect quite brilliantly: "Close echo heats the woodman's axe / To double on it, as in glee / With clap of hands, and little lacks / Of meaning in her repartee."

11. Søren Kierkegaard, *Either / Or,* trans. D. F. Swenson and L. M. Swenson, rev. H. A. Johnson (New York, 1959), I, 23, 33.

is misread as the literal, even as an image of voice is mistaken for a vocal presence. And yet, as both voice and echo are sound, the literal dimension—whose possibility Nietzsche denies in this essay on "Truth and Falsity in an Ultramoral Sense"—and the figurative one are both language. [12]

Language answering language, then—questions returned to questions, like George Meredith's "The whither whose echo is whence" ("A Faith on Trial"), or answers to answers or even texts answering texts—characterizes the later phases of the transubstantiation of echoed voice. [13] It is inevitable that the trope of echo should come to stand for crucial questions about poetic language itself. Pushkin's Echo hears natural noises, horns, voices of shepherds and maidens, and answers them all, but is never answered in return. Such, he insists, is the nature of the poet as well ("Echo," 1831). It is even more inevitable that the delay between prior voice and responding echo in acoustical actuality should become in naturalized romantic mythology a trope of diachrony, of the distance between prior and successive poems. In a later poem on "The Mountain Echo" (1814), Wordsworth suggests that poems themselves, like the voice of the bird in the opening stanza, raise questions in, and of, the surrounding hills. He concludes that

> Yes, we have
> Answers and we know not whence;
> Echoes from beyond the grave,
> Recognized intelligence!

12. I quote the translation of M. A. Mügge reprinted in *The Philosophy of Nietzsche,* ed. Geoffrey Clive (New York, 1965), 510.

13. In Samuel Johnson's *Rambler* essay (No. 121) on imitation, young men are called "echoes." In Blake's *The Four Zoas,* Plate 13, "Demons of waves their watry Eccho's wake," and the conceit may as well touch on sound propagation through a medium as on the pictorialization of sound. In *Adonais,* echo "pined away / Into a shadow of all sounds"—Shelley here revises the "image of voice" into a kind of spectre.

> Such rebounds our inward ear
> Catches sometimes from afar. . . .

It is as if the ordinary, or outward, ear may hear histories, accounts, quotations or even allusions from the poetry of the past.[14] But the oracular function of the higher versions of the mythologized echo occurs in texts where more is heard that meets the eye. Andrew Marvell's "echoing song" would only echo hollowly to the unhearing skull in a grave; but it remains (in his "Coy Mistress" poem) echoing in the textual sense outside of and beyond the grave, long after both lovers are dead. The "terraced echoes, prostrate on the plain" of Hart Crane's vision of reawakening eloquence (in "The Broken Tower") lie momentarily open to reveal themselves as chronologically successive layers of poetic voice. Ovid's nymph vanished into voice; the natural fact of disembodied voice vanishes, in a later stage of things, into text. It is this era in the mythological history of echo which supplies our commonly employed literary historical metaphor of allusive "echo" that is the subject of this study and which, first within, and then between, texts we shall now proceed to consider.

14. Elsewhere, for Wordsworth, the figurative or internalized echo can improve upon or augment the source: "My own voice chear'd me, and, far more, the mind's / Internal echo of the imperfect sound." For an elaborate discussion of Wordsworthian echo, with particular reference to my treatment of it, see Geoffrey Hartman, "Words, Wish Worth: Wordsworth," in *Deconstruction and Criticism* (New York, 1979), 177–213.

III.
Echo Schematic

The remainder of this book will concern another stage in the
mythography of Echo. Here the demystified nymph
(whether mourning in tangled thickets like all the other
nymphs who, in Milton's Christmas ode, became tropes at
the birth of Christ, or depersonified by acoustical theory
and empiricism) reemerges figuratively in text, rather than
in sound. Recognizing her there is itself a metaphor of hearing, for texts are haunted by echoes. Just as the myth of the
nymph inspired a range of moralizations—from mocking,
affirming, and haunting to the early modernist sense of
writing poetry itself—so there exist within, and across,
texts a range of relations between voice and echo as they
appear in various verbal patterns and schemes.

Echoing becomes a canonical formal scheme even before
Ovid's use of it in his fable in the *Metamorphoses*. The celebrated earliest example is in an epigram of Callimachus,[1] all
the more interesting for contemporary theory because of its
associations of erotic possession with textuality, voice, and
contingent presence: "I hate the cyclic poem [that passes
from mouth to mouth], I have no love for the heavily trav-

1. Actually, there are two prior instances. The echo scene in Euripides'
lost *Andromeda* was itself allusively "echoed" by Aristophanes in the *The-
mophoriazusae,* in mockery of Euripides. In the latter play, Mnesilochus,
Euripides' uncle, is bound by hostile women; acting out a travesty of
Andromeda's being chained to her rock, he calls upon Echo, who answers
him in fragments of Euripides' play. One tradition has it that the actor
playing Euripides doubled as Echo, underlining the mockery. But Echo's
returns (lines 1069–96) are simple, unrevised repetitions of what has been
said, with no trace of wordplay. Callimachus' poem initiates the echo
scheme or ironic revision. The translations, except when otherwise indi-
cated, are my own.

elled road; I abhor a beloved who wanders about and I don't
drink from a fountain: all public things (*demosia*) disgust
me." It is in the final couplet that the echo effect occurs,
when the poem makes its gesture toward possession, pri-
vacy, and original beauty, only to have it fall back into the
realm of the *demosia* again. Lysanias (his name means "re-
liever of sorrow") is proclaimed to be beautiful, but the very
act of utterance loses him: "Lysanias, you're truly fair, fair;
but before I can get this out clearly, echo says 'Someone else
has him.' " The conventional formula of praise for beauty,
"naichi kalos, kalos," is echoed by the "allos" ("other,"
"someone else"). Whether we think of echo as revealing
the *allos* lurking in every lover's assured cry of *kalos,* or
whether, as one scholar has suggested,[2] the whole phrase
"naichi kalos" would come back as the echoing "exei allos,"
the revisionary effect of the echo is apparent. In this milieu
of echoing, it is as if the empty, formulaic repetition of *kalos,
kalos,* and the scattered near homophones—*alla* ("but") and
allos, êcho ("echo") and *echei* ("has")—were at work to rein-
force the interpretive, mocking effect of the echo's phonetic
mimicry.

Callimachus' epigram is not the *locus classicus* of the literary device of echo, however; it is Ovid's use of it in his story
of Echo and Narcissus that is most familiar. It is there that
the poet dramatizes the failed erotic encounter between the

2. W. R. Paton in his Loeb edition of *The Greek Anthology,* Vòl IV.
Another editor, G. R. Mair, suggests that emended punctuation would
give "but before Echo can get this out clearly, someone says 'he's another's.'" In either case, the echo effect works with an analytic irony.
Despite the possible polemical role of this epigram—against the school of
Pergamon, praising cyclic epics like Apollonius Rhodius' *Argonautica* at the
expense of "moderns" like Callimachus himself—the erotic and the poetic
generally are mutually allegorized in what may be a more profound poem
than its familiarity suggests. The precise effect of the echo is very hard to
get in English translation. I should venture, for the last lines, the following:
"But you, my own Lysanias, are fairer than all flowers. / —'*Ours!*' say a
hundred echoes hard upon my words, 'He's *ours!*'"

two by literally transcribing Echo's fragmentary resoundings of the youth's terminal syllables: "Huc coeamus" ("here
let us meet"), and she—never happier to answer—responds
"coeamus" (in its other sense of "let us make love"—we
might get the effect in English by translating "Here let us
come together," answered by Echo's "Let us come. Together."). And so forth. But when she rushes up to embrace
him at last, the young man doomed to love himself only
flees her, and fleeing, cries out to her to unhand him: " 'emo-
riar, quam sit tibi copia nostri' " ("may I die before I give
you power over me"). She responds " 'sit tibi copia nostri' "
("I give you power over me"), and nothing more. Whereas
in the earlier instances in this passage (*Metamorphoses* III,
380–92) the echoing phrase betokens some agreement (as
with "coeamus" above), in the last case a telling irony results from the repetition, for the reference of the pronouns
has changed. Echo is in fact saying that henceforth the ini-
tiating speaker will have power over her (in tract of time it
will mean to provide her with *copia* and copy). Even though
Ovid gives a very different account of the origins of Echo's
mimicry, he chooses the Narcissus episode, and not the
scene in which she talked Juno to distraction, for dramatic
representation. The self-descriptive force of Echo's answer
(by saying *only* [*nihil nisi*] "I give you power over me," she
thereby gives the power) is itself delicately resonant.

Ovid makes us feel that Narcissus, who mocked (*luserat*)
all overtures of companionship, is appropriately treated by
the nymph. And yet her responses to him are far from
mocking. They partake of the amplification which we see
earlier in Bion's *Lament for Adonis:*

> I bewail Adonis: "Ended is lovely Adonis;"
> "—Ded is lovely Adonis," the Loves all rebewail me
>
> Aiadzôton Adônin. "apôleto kalos Adônis."
> "ôleto kalos Adônis" epaindzousin Erôtes.

The chorus of affirmation here is a typical, truncated echo response. The verb *apollumi* ("utterly destroyed") has its prefix chopped off to give the ordinarily weaker, but here more evocative, *ollumi* ("killed"). The refrain of the whole lament—"I bewail Adonis: the Loves all rebewail me"—is compounded from the first two lines and contains within it the affirmative response. It is significant that, later on in the same poem, a chorus of pastoral plaint for Aphrodite's sorrow is made to echo her own wail for her lover; finally, the whole isle of Cythera, hills and dales, sings out sadly:

> "Waly-o Cytherea, ended is lovely Adonis"
> And Echo sings in answer: "Ended is lovely Adonis"

By this means, the echoing device of the opening lines, the refrain, and the choiring wails of nature are identified with the patronness of the device, Echo herself.

The device—or scheme, as I shall refer to it—is shown in Bion's elegy in both its strict and applied or extended forms. The strict form is the well-known one which has descended through the centuries. In it, questions are asked of, or propositions addressed to, Echo, in successive lines of verse; either she completes the line by echoing the last syllable or two, or her response makes up a separate short line. Whenever possible, her fragmentary response involves a pun or other alteration of sense. From an epigram by the Byzantine Guaradas in the *Greek Anthology,* up through much Renaissance lyric and epigrammatic verse, the form tended toward the satiric. Usually regarded as the Renaissance original of the mode is a little dialogue by Politian between Pan and Echo (1498); in Italy many others followed, and in England, after George Gascoigne's introduction of it in *The Princely Pleasures* at Kenilworth Castle (1575).

The scheme can, of course, operate in prose as well as in verse, although examples such as that of Erasmus' colloquy, *Echo,* are rare. This latter is distinguished for the brilliance of its punning. A dialogue between a youth and a learned echo on the subject of studies, it frequently plays between Greek and Latin—thus, the youth's "decem iam annos aetatem trivi in Cicerone" ("I've spent ten years on Cicero") is echoed, in Greek, "one!" ("ass!"), as "Ciceronianus" ("a Ciceronian") shrinks in echo to "anous" ("madman"), or as "Musarum studia" ("the Muses' studies") are revealed in Greek echo as "dia" ("divine ones"). In its more usual Latin responses, the echo plucks "otium" out of "sacerdotium" and, impatient with the dull student at the end of the dialogue, answers his irritated "non me delectant sermones dissylabi" ("I don't like words of two syllables") with "abi" ("go away") and, after that, his "proinde si me voles abire, dicito" ("Well, if you want me to go, say so") with "ito" ("Go!"), as if the student had meant something like "dic-'ito' " in the first place.

Politian, Tasso (more elaborately and elegantly), and many others all employ this kind of satiric fragmentation, in which the breaking apart of a longer word or phrase is literally and figuratively "reductive," and by which a contrary or self-emending meaning is shown to have been implicit in the original affirmation. Echo's power is thus one of being able to reveal the implicit, and if she is oracular it is in a way which demythologizes all the oracles: "Chi dara fine al gran dolore?" ("Who will put an end to this great sadness?") asks the primary voice in Daniele Barbaro's little poem, and Echo answers "l'ore" ("the hours passing"); "Echo! What shall I do to my Nymph when I go to behold her?" and Barnabe Barnes' Echo answers the lover "Hold her!" with all of the low-erotic reductiveness of a Donne elegy. Elbridge Colby, in *The Echo-Device in Literature* (1920), listed and commented on a multitude of such echo poems (including texts by Sidney, Watson, Drayton, Herbert of Cherbury, Cowley, Shirley, and others in French and Italian as well) and saw no particular relation between the "device" and any rhetorical complexity. And yet the difference is vast between the satiric returns of early French echoes which plucked the *avoir* out of *savoir* or, from *la chose plus infame,* the inevitable *femme* or Swift's "What most moves women when we them address?—Echo: A dress," on the one hand, and George Herbert's "Heaven," on the other.

> O who will show me these delights on high?
> > *Echo, I.*
> Thou Echo, thou art Mortall, all men know.
> > *Echo, No.*
> Wert thou not born among the trees and leaves?
> > *Echo, Leaves.*
> And are there any leaves that still abide?
> > *Echo, Bide.*
> What leaves are they? Impart the matter wholly.
> > *Echo, Holy.*
> Are holy leaves the Echo then of blisse?
> > *Echo, Yes.*
> Then tell me, what is the supreme delight?
> > *Echo, Light.*
> Light to the minde; what shall the will enjoy?
> > *Echo, Joy.*
> But are there cares and businesse with the pleasure?
> > *Echo, Leisure?*
> Light, joy and leisure; but shall they persever?
> > *Echo, Ever.*

Here it is not only the expansive—rather than reductive—nature of the puns (wholly/holy, etc.), but the very transformation of both the myth and the scheme that is at stake. The "leaves," among which we may expect to find the Ovidian nymph and her echo device descendants lurking together, become manifestly transfigured into the leaves of the holy book, just half-way through the poem. The *bide* extracted from *abide* is an imperative to the reader to await the completed turning of the trope. The extractions of *light,*

joy, and *leisure* from the longer words is part of the extrac-
tion of a sacred poetry from an erotic or otherwise secular
poetic language, a process Herbert is always writing about.
The nymph, the device, and its rhetoric are all transformed
when the speaker's voice rebounds not from an Ovidian
grot or a pastoral spot, but from the open cave of the scriptural page. Echo becomes not only holy, but writ.[3]

Gascoigne's Kenilworth masque presented an actual encounter with the persona of the nymph, following three
other manifestations during the course of the entertain-
ments' two days—she was preceded by Sibilla in an arbor,
the Lady of the Lake emerging from water, and "a savage
man, all in Ivie." The last of these inquires of the audience
why there are such festivities; he learns nothing from them,
and concludes "Wel Eccho, where art thou, could I but
Eccho finde / She would returne me answer yet by blast of
every winde." The problem—and this initiates a convention for dramatic scenes of this sort, at least in English—is to
find where Echo dwells; she solves it by her first rebound of
"Here," and then continues in the usual pattern of repetitions at the end of questions, etc. Her answers are all
affirmative and literal: she is asked "A or B," and echoes
back "B," and so forth. The one exception is a little emblematic tribute, inserted in the exchanges, to the Earl of Leices-
ter, provider of the scene and festivities:

> And who gave all these gifts? I pray thee (*Eccho*) say?
> Was it not he? who (but of late) this building ere did lay?
>
> *Eccho.*   *Dudley.*

But it is clearly in violation of the literal rebounds of the rest
of the scene, stuck into it like arms in a cartouche in the sky
above a battle scene.

---

3. Cf. also the pruning down of words (e.g., *charm*/*harm*/*arm*) in Herbert's "Paradise."

Whether named or not, the ghost of the nymph Echo can reappear figuratively in echo songs, in which echo schemes in verse are set to music. Politian's influential poem was set to music by Heinrich Isaac in the first quarter of the sixteenth century, and echo madrigals by Marenzio, Lassus, Vecchi, A. Gabrieli, and Praetorius, and operatic scenes by Peri, Monteverdi, Rossi, Cavalli, Draghi, Alessandro Scarlatti, and others were common. Particularly in the baroque period, contrasting dynamics allowed for a conventional pianissimo repetition of the echoing phrase. Whether or not the personified echoer was identified with one of the vocal lines, the actual musical voice would generate a presence. In English music, Purcell's echo chorus in *Dido and Aeneas* ("In our deep-vaulted cell / The charm we'll prepare") is sung by witches engaged in "Too dreadful a practice / For the open air," and gives a gothic touch to the ambiance. In *The Fairy Queen,* Dryden wrote in a passage of echoing that, far from presenting Echo as even a momentary personage, allows for the musical setting of a figuration of her presence: "While Eccho shall in sounds remote / Repeat each note, each note, each note." Purcell's song moves through three degrees of diminution ("loud," "soft," "softer") in the final repeats; the composer then confirms the purely musical basis of the effect by appending an instrumental echo piece for drums, hautboys, and continuo. The sheer musical mimesis of acoustical echo was enhanced by means of the terraced dynamics of later baroque music and the seventeenth-century vogue for echo stops on organs. Aside from the complex role of echo in later music, both attest to the continuing formal, somewhat trivial, survival of echo as a baroque structural element we might call "again, but softer."[4]

4. Later musical uses of echo include those in the Bach *Christmas Oratorio,* Berlioz' *Requiem,* etc. Milton Babbitt's Philomel (1962) carries both the

The echo device, then, may be embodied in epigram or song or dramatic scene. Potentially, it can augment and trope the utterance it echoes, as well as reduce and ridicule; it can even serve a semantically redundant and more purely "musical" function, one which we associate with certain types of refrain. The refrain of Bion's lament for Adonis, although Theocritan in tradition, "evolves"—according to the local ad hoc fiction of the poem's own generation—from echoic patterns. Indeed, we might invent a myth of the First Refrain in which the originators played the parts of echoing nymphs. I should like at this point to consider some traditionally identified schemes and patterns of repetition in poetry as informal occurrences of echoing. The nymph de-mythologized and depersonified comes to inhabit texts—even the wholly fallen leaves for which Herbert's holy scrip-tural ones are a kind of model. But this is not only a question of the relative formality of the pattern, any more than it turns on the presence of a persona of Echo herself. It is a matter of rhetoric.

Aside from the manifest formal structure of the echo song, in which a rhetorical echo is embodied in a personified answerer or mocker, the scheme of echoing covers a wide array of sorts of controlled repetition of word or phrase. Starting from the micro-linguistic level of phonology, we should properly have to consider such phenomena as redu-plication, alliteration, assonance, and full rhyme as regions of Echo's empire. Nevertheless, when such devices become schematic or definitive for a poetic convention, their rela-tion to echo diminishes (e.g., the lack of expressiveness or evocation of alliterative pairs of words in Old English). On the other hand, when a repetitive scheme is momentarily emptied of meaning, the phonetic pattern becomes more

---

poetic scheme and the musical device a stage further; see my *Vision and Resonance* (New York and London, 1976), 301 –3.

like an echoing rebound: *rime riche,* underlined by syllabic stress accent in English, seems to us to echo hollowly, and seems somehow flat and inept (even in Chaucer, in whom its use comes from no poverty). French, with its lack of syllabic stress, has been able to play more echoically with homophones in verse than has English. The use of such devices runs from the fifteenth-century *rhétoriqueurs* to Mallarmé, from Jean Molinet's "Molinet n'est sans bruit ne sans nom, non; / Il a son son et comme tu vois, voix. . . ." to the *rime equivoquée,* as it is called, of such perfectly punning echoings as Théodore de Banville's "Dans ces meubles laques, rideaux et dais moroses, / Danse, aime, bleu laquais, ris d'oser des mot roses." It is in another, but analogous, sense that echo, too, equivocates.

Totally programmatic schemes of resonance, however, come to seem more and more like reiterative beats of a metronome or a drum. In a conventionally patterned pair of sounds, like *tick-tock* (and a purely fictional one—there is no alteration of pitch in the successive sounds of a clock escapement or of a pendulum), the second does indeed, in Romance and Germanic languages, at least, appear to partake of resonance. The back vowel (*dong*) seems the echo of the front one (*ding*).

Pairs or triads of slightly varied sounds are shaded with echo in certain allusive contexts. One of these is the sequence of variations that resemble noun or adjective declensions, the recitation of grammatical paradigms in Indo-European. Wallace Stevens, who performs a Miltonic, perhaps an almost Heideggerian, turn on the etymology of *decline,* invokes acoustical echoes in "Le Monocle de Mon Oncle" as "declensions of their jingling bells." He makes the connection the other way in the paradigm of paradigms: "Pipperoo, pippera, pipperum . . . the rest is rot." (The last two words of the line recapitulate the front-vowel/back-vowel echo scheme of the mock declension.) A Miltonic prologue to just this scheme can be found in Adam's lament at the end of *Paradise Lost,* Book IX, where he invokes Eve: "How art thou lost, how on a sudden lost, / Defac't, deflow'r'd, and now to Death devote." Milton frequently makes schemes and even puns of prefixes and other secondary morphemes. Consider the sequence from earlier in Book IX (lines 6–9), where the putative prefix *dist*—— seems to acquire meaning throughout the carefully balanced sequence:

> . . . foul distrust, and breach
> Disloyal on the part of Man, revolt,
> And disobedience: on the part of Heav'n
> Now alienated, distance and distaste

(And here, as throughout *Paradise Lost,* we may notice how much the assonances at "*breach* / diso*bed*ience" and"*al*ienat*e*d / dis*taste*," occurring, like the rhymes in that poem, in no regular pattern, partake of echo.)

The traditional rhetorical schemes that partake of echo include various figures of repetition such as *epistrophe,* with its repetition of word or phrase in successive cadential positions; *epanalepsis,* or of initial clausal word by final one (George Puttenham, in his 1589 *Arte of English Poesie* calls this "Eccho sounde" or "slow returne"), and the *anadiplosis,* so famously used in Sir Philip Sidney's first sonnet from *Astrophel and Stells.*[5] The reflexive schemes—*antimetabole* and *chiasmus*—on the other hand, seem less to generate echo than the others (e.g., "Can make a Heav'n of Hell, a Hell of Heaven," where the reversal of syntactic group is more prominent than the repetition of words). A mountain echo

5. There are also *diaphora, ploce,* and *epizeuxis,* which Puttenham calls "the underlay or cuckoo-spell" and illustrates with a couplet he ascribes to Raleigh: "With wisdomes eyes had but blind fortune seene, / Then had my loove, my loove for ever beene." Of these three figures, this last partakes most of echo.

that gave back a perfect acoustical palindrome would not be perceived as an *echo,* but as some enigmatic, perhaps oracular, *answer.*

The most important scheme of echo, however, is the refrain. The very word is associated with echo, being cognate with *refract* (but from Old French *refraindre,* with a sense of breaking back or again). Certainly some notion inheres of a broken-off part of a longer lyric unit, whether in the burden of the medieval carol (which might often be in Latin, with the verse in the vernacular) or in recurrent lines or half-lines in some of the more elaborate Romance lyric forms. In oral poetry, refrain frequently has the function of choral assent: a leader will sing a series of strophes, and a chorus of followers will repeat a refrain, often to provide thereby the music for their own bout of physical work or dancing. The rhetorical relation between strophe and refrain is one of affirmation and perhaps implementation. But as in the realm of echo, the prior voice produces new *copia* or verbal substance (resulting from memory or improvisation), while the refrain returns. Even though two voices are involved, however, the voice of refrain echoes itself, across the gap of the leading voice's interjections, although a burden or refrain may be originally introduced at the close of an initial strophe. Depending upon the oral genre—work song, ritual dance, etc.—the very return of the refrain may be a trope for "that bit's over: let's get on with it," or "now we get to sing our part again."

In the general metamorphosis of voice into text that occurs in the history of lyrical poetry, refrains develop another attribute of echo: decay or diminution. Mere reiteration can lessen significance; there are indeed semantic situations that reflect the crudities of information theory, and in which predictability and redundancy are clearly identified. A refrain occurring in a long narrative ballad, for example, can be—and usually is—printed as "etc." in modern editions.

The longer the ballad, the more the return of the refrain comes to approximate the condition of the textless music, and of semantic pause. The conventionalized singing or laughter of the "fal-la-la" and "nonny-nonny-no" refrains marks one extreme of a spectrum of significance. The other is represented by the refrain that constantly varies in significance with puns, new syntactic or other referential contexts, etc., at each occurrence. (The handling of the refrain lines in modern villanelles is an example.) By and large, all refrains can be easily distributed along such a spectrum of altered significance, just as echoes might be so arranged for their relative hollowness or plenitude of verbal power. And as with actual refrains, so with the refrain-like schemes mentioned earlier, and so with verse forms with predictable repetitions used for linkage—coronas of sonnets, the *rimes couronnées* of Clément Marot, redoubling *rondeaux,* and the like.

Of all the schematic forms that Echo inhabits, the sestina is perhaps the richest; its power comes from refrain itself being broken into single recurring words and from the particular, literal resounding of the terminal word of each stanza in the initial line ending of the next one. There is more in a sestina than a ghost of figurative echoing in the stanzaic repetitions: such ghosts are obscured by the more acoustical echo of adjacent lines, themselves spaced out sufficiently so as to modulate an otherwise incessant, and inevitably trivial, pounding. But the rhetorical activity of the initial line of each stanza overpowers the fading voice of echo, to double and redouble a new word over the old one, rather than letting the decrescendo of repetition occur. In Rossetti's translation of Dante's "Stony Sestina," this occurs with greatest force toward the end:

> A while ago, I saw her dressed in green,—
> So fair, she might have wakened in a stone

> This love which I do feel even for her shade;
> And therefore, as one woos a graceful lady,
> I wooed her in a field that was all grass
> Girdled about with very lofty hills.
>
> Yet shall the streams turn back and climb the hills
> Before Love's flame in this damp wood and green
> Burn, as it burns within a youthful lady,
> For my sake, who would sleep away in stone
> My life, or feed like beasts upon the grass,
> Only to see her garments cast a shade.

Refrain becomes more than scheme in the later history of lyric poetry, when "song" becomes only figuratively so, and poetry lives in the metaphorical music of its own schematic patterns of sound and momentary meaning. Refrains can become figurative in many ways, but most of these depend upon allusion to more literal occurrences of them. Those in Yeats' later lyrics are a good example of this; in the case of "John Kinsella's Lament for the Late Mary Moore," the famous refrain (*"What shall I do for pretty girls / Now my old bawd is dead?"*) actually generated the poem, in a complex refiguration of the relation of verse and burden in medieval song. A most instructive view of secondary or figurative refrain—indeed, of poetic refrain as echo of refrains of the past—is seen in Wallace Stevens' "Autumn Refrain," itself a poem of broken repetitions and echoing fragments.

We might dwell for a moment on one of the most famous fragments of broken refrain in our literature, the nonce burden in Keats' "Ode to a Nightingale" following the mention of the "perilous seas in faery lands forlorn" (70). The next strophe begins "Forlorn! the very word is like a bell / To toll me back from thee to my sole self!" (71–72). The echoing repetition returns, as has often been observed, another sense of the word *forlorn,* as if some of the perils of the seas lay in the fragility of the vision which they helped compose. The word is, even here, Miltonic, with its resounding of a literal and a figurative meaning. It recalls Adam's sense of life without Eve in Paradise: "To live again in these wild Woods forlorn" (*Paradise Lost* IX, 910), where the last word trails away in a cloud of sad prophetic irony: "these wild Woods forlorn" are not the wilderness of fallen nature. Adam thinks he means Eden figuratively, but he is, alas, literally invoking both the fallen world and the lost unfallen one: his trope of the place of loss is an unwittingly literal designation of the loss of place. Keats' "forlorn" is like a very echo from within his text, but it reaches back to another voice behind it.

The scheme of refrain is likewise linked to the echo of affirmation and acknowledgment that we have already remarked in Hesiod, pastoral tradition, and so forth, in the mythopoeic account of its origination in *Paradise Lost*. The First Hymn (V, 153–208) invokes heavenly powers for aid in amplification of its praising voice, even as the Lady invokes Echo's amplification in *Comus*. But the unfallen hymn of praise transcends the *anaphora* and catalogue of its precursor Psalm 148 by seeming to generate its refrain— indeed, the very idea of refrain—during the course of its unfolding. Before moving on from echoing schemes to ad hoc tropes of echo, we might examine the Original Refrain in detail.

Adam and Eve (V, 147–52) are in Paradise

> to praise
>
> > Thir Maker, in fit strains pronounct or sung
> > Unmeditated, such prompt eloquence
> > Flow'd from thir lips, in Prose or numerous Verse,
> > More tuneable than needed Lute or Harp
> > To add more sweetness

—or, as we might continue, to add more of the significance which Schopenhauer felt, and Nietzsche quoted him as feeling, accompanying instrumental music gave to utterance and action. Adam and Eve's language, we are implicitly told, needed no supplementary *ethos* or *pathos,* and certainly none of the *logos* which, for romantic thought, purely instrumental music came to embody as well.

In this total *a capella* song, classical and unfallen, the original pair first observe—echoing, *sotto voce,* Psalm 19—that even God's "lowest works" "declare / Thy goodness beyond thought, and Power Divine" (V, 158–59). Then they move into the imperative, hortatory mode of the hymn which follows. They call for the "Sons of Light" to "speak," thus reversing the great pattern of fallen praise (in Pindar's first Pythian Ode, and in the myth of the statue of Memnon) in which light strikes a figurative echo in literal sound from a body, instead of merely casting a shadow: "Thou Sun, of this great World both Eye and Soul, / Acknowledge him thy Greater, sound his praise / In thy eternal course" (V, 171–73).

This is the hymn's own primary voice. Its first *Nachklang* is picked up tentatively, across an enjambment which cuts the amplifying echo, the distant *epistrophe,* in half:

> Moon, that now meet'st the orient Sun, now fli'st
> With the first Stars, fixt in thir Orb that flies,
> And yee five other wand'ring Fires that move
> In mystic Dance not without Song, resound
> His praise, who out of Darkness call'd up Light.
> (V, 175–79)

Adam, who will soon himself call up Sound out of Silence, then establishes the formula / (verb) + "his praise" / in the second half of the significantly varied end-stopped lines that grow into the refrain of the remainder of the hymn:

> Air, and ye Elements of eldest birth
> Of Nature's Womb, that in quaternion run
> Perpetual Circle, multiform, and mix

And nourish all things, let your ceaseless change
Vary to our great Maker still new praise.

Ye Mists and Exhalations that now rise
From Hill or steaming Lake, dusky or grey,
Till the Sun paint your fleecy skirts with Gold,
In honor to the World's great Author rise,
Whether to deck with Clouds th'uncolor'd sky,
Or wet the thirsty Earth with falling showers,
Rising or falling still advance his praise.

His praise ye Winds, that from four Quarters blow,
Breathe soft or loud; and wave your tops, ye Pines,
With every Plant, in sign of Worship wave.
Fountains and yee, that warble as ye flow,
Melodious murmurs, warbling tune his praise.

Join voices all ye living Souls; ye Birds,
That singing up to Heaven Gate ascend,
Bear on your wings and in your notes his praise;

Yee that in Waters glide, and yee that walk
The Earth, and stately tread, or lowly creep;
Witness if I be silent, Morn or Even,
To Hill, or Valley, Fountain or fresh shade
Made vocal by my Song, and taught his praise.

(V, 180–204)

This is not glossed by the narration as "the First Refrain," but such, indeed, it is. Like the famous "cras amet qui numquam amavit, quiquam amavit cras amet" line of the *Pervigilium Veneris* ("tomorrow those who have never loved will love, and those who have will love tomorrow"), the broken echo concludes, and builds up, "stanzas" of various lengths, summing up the essential qualities of the different choral voices. The elements "vary" the praise, as the rest of the hymn will "vary" the refrain. Thus, the "Mists and Exhalations," "Rising or falling still advance his praise" (with an echo of "still" from line 184); then the lovely anadiplosis of line 192, where the winds pick up the motion of the clouds, transmit it to the visible waving of the trees, and complete a traditional symphony of the *locus amoenus* with the warbling of the water's eloquence, followed by the bird song.[6]

The final stanza (200–204) returns to the singers themselves. A *tornata* that, like the conclusion of *Lycidas,* frames as well as completes, it is self-referential. Its self-reference is like that of the prayer, which concludes in a kind of caudal or meta-prayer for its own efficacy (and which, in Herbert's poems in *The Temple,* is frequently disposed throughout the main text in a constant figurative undersong). In addition, it invokes the primary world of pastoral. The sounding landscape is "made vocal" by poetry by means of that primary animation which, for Vico, is the "most luminous" of tropes, in that it makes fables of the inanimate by giving "sense and passion" to things, here both embodied in voice. The authenticity of the hymn itself is here avowedly confined to a realm of figure: all that can bear witness to unfallen man's praising voice are the stock fictions of pastoral fable, "taught" his praise. This echoes Virgil's first eclogue, "formosam resonare doces Amaryllida in silvas," even as they are both reechoed, in fallen modulations, in Adam's forlorn cry in Book X (860–62):

> O Woods, O Fountains, Hillocks, Dales and Bow'rs,
> With other echo late I taught your Shades
> To answer, and resound far other Song.

Adam here is already like Virgil's Tityrus and the "starv'd lover" of Book IV, line 769. Even the Original Song is full of

6. A historical origination of literary refrain is to be found in that locus of echo, pastoral tradition. Theocritus' *Idyll* I generates a refrain which, in its successive versions, grows self-reflexive: "Begin a country-song, dear Muses, begin to sing" changes to "Begin a country-song, Muses, again begin to sing" and, finally, to "Leave off your country-song, Muses, leave off your singing." For the role of repetitive form in pastoral, see the excellent discussion in Thomas G. Rosenmeyer, *The Green Cabinet* (Berkeley, Los Angeles and London, 1969), 93–95.

echoes, although in *Paradise Lost,* an internal *Nachklang* frequently generates a proleptic *Vorklang,* or preecho. In the poem's pattern of unfallen organization, we must take this hymn to be the true *locus amoenus* (Milton's *locus classicus*) of pastoral echo, and its rhetoric to be that of pastoral praise, not loss.

But perhaps the most remarkable aspect of the scheme of echoing refrain here is that it is employed tropically. The first "echo" of the series which increases, rather than diminishes, in significatory volume is itself a metaphor of the reflection of light. The sun (as Conti says, "author of light to the other stars") "sounds / His praise"; the other heavenly bodies "resound / His praise" in echo, and in conceptual parallel to their return of solar light.

The Original Hymn, then, manifests not only the First Refrain, but the First Echo.[7] Even the angelic choir's "sacred Song" in Book III (372–415) has no refrain, nor indeed any other echoing schemes. It is like sung doctrine, and requires the accompaniment of "Harps ever tun'd, that glittering by thir side / Like Quivers hung"—that is, aside from the shade of pun on "quaver" as musical ornament, harps with strings like the glittering arrows of erotic putti. It concludes with the neoclassical lyric formula "never shall my Harp thy praise / Forget." The only natural acoustical echoes occurring previously in *Paradise Lost* are in the demonic regions of

---

7. But not the first mocking echo: see *Paradise Lost* II, 789. The blending of echo into refrain or refrainlike repetition can be seen in the strange hexameters of Abraham Fraunces's *The Third Part of the Countess of Pembroke's Yvychurch* (1592). Here is part of the metamorphosis of the nymph Echo:

> Yea, very bones at last, were made to be stones: the resounding
> Voyce, and onely the voyce of forelorne *Eccho* remaineth:
> *Eccho* remaineth a voyce, in deserts *Eccho* remaineth,
> *Eccho* noe-where seene, heard every where by the deserts.
>
> (Ei_v)

Book II, where they are used in carefully turned figures to describe the nature of damned assent. The fallen angels agreeing with Mammon after his speech produce a sound likened to that of winds stored in hollow rocks, played back later "with hoarse cadence" to "lull" anchored ships (284–90). But we must remember that this concord will only lead to the full disclosure of its own acoustic nature in the transformed hisses later on (Book X). And so, too, with the assent given to Satan's words further on:

> If chance the radiant Sun with farewell sweet
> Extend his ev'ning beam, the fields revive,
> The birds thir notes renew, and bleating herds
> Attest thir joy, that hill and valley rings.
>
> (II, 492–95)

(Here, too, light strikes forth sound, and "herds" half-echo "birds.") But this very simile, his epic need to use it, and its lamentable success in the poem cause Milton to interject, in one of those rare moments of intrusion, his revulsion. In Book IV, he cries out "Honor dishonorable" in disgust at the notion that postlapsarian *pudeur* about nudity was present in Paradise. Here in Book II, he cries out: "O shame to men! Devil with Devil damn'd / Firm concord holds, men only disagree." Both this damnable echoing and the unechoing, unfigured music of the heavenly choir in Book III, then, are recalled and transcended in their echoes in the First Hymn. They are cancelled and transformed in a process analogous in Milton to what Hegel calls *Aufhebung*.

The Original Hymn not only originates refrain, but interprets the scheme as a trope of echo—as assent, consent, concert, consonance, approval, and witness. Moreover, its relation to older utterances of the trope is itself resonant. This affirmative aspect of echo's figure completely obliterates a negative, mocking one, which appears in a starkly literal way earlier, again in the demonic milieu of Book II.

Sin's account to Satan of her parturition of Death concludes as her son, "he my inbred enemy," "forth issu'd, brandishing his fatal Dart / Made to destroy." The following lines are strongly Ovidian: "I fled, and cri'd out *Death*; / Hell trembl'd at the hideous Name, and sigh'd / From all her Caves, and back resounded *Death*" (II, 787–89).

This is an instance of a negation more profound than even the reductive mockery which Milton draws upon, and Sin anticipates for fallen human poetry. She cries out her son's name in a blend of erotic fear and mother love; she names him directly and screams out the general human alarm (as in "Murder!"). Hell's return of the word is the sound of revulsion from caves whose hollowed emptiness has now for the first time been (1) employed as a physical locus of echo, and (2) figuratively identified with negation, nonbeing, and death. And yet the whole event uses the materials of pastoral affirmative echo, perverted in the Satanic mode of eternally twisted tropings. "The forest wide is fitter to resound / The hollow Echo of my carefull cryes" says Spenser's Cuddie in his sestina (*Shepheardes Calender,* "August," 159–60), thus importing the hollowness of the nymph's abode into the sound of all the body she has left.[8] But most poetic echoes are far from hollow; rather are they crowded with sound and rebound or, like Milton's echo of "Death," with dialectic. Never again would negative echo resound so immediately and so clearly. In American poetry from Emerson through Whitman, Frost, and Stevens, the seascape or land-

8. The sestina is, as we have seen, a most resounding form, and Cuddie's expressly so; consider how the lines quoted above (from strophe 2) echo the opening lines of the first strophe: "Ye wastefull woods beare witnesse of my woe / Wherein my plaints did oftentimes resound"—as those plaints indeed just have resounded in the alliterations of the previous lines: "Ye careless birds are privie to my cryes / Which in your songs were wont to take a part." Spenser continually glosses his echoes by identifying them with meaningful sound.

scape will only be able to utter the word *death* in a barely decipherable whisper.

The comic or satiric echo song depends for its force, then, on the dramatic irony sustained by the primary voice's not "hearing," as it were, the nasty synecdochic echo (else it would surely, we feel, shut up after a couplet or two). An even stronger dramatic irony is generated when the speaker is made inadvertently to echo a prior voice: dramatic form is an implicit echo chamber in this respect. (One has only to think of the role of words like *natural* and *nature* in *King Lear* or *honest* in *Othello,* whose reboundings define the tragic contingencies of those who give them voice. The operation of the trope of dramatic irony in such cases seems dialectical. Is it because of the anterior enunciations of such words that a tragic hero is known to all but himself as an echoer, rather than as a propounder? Or does the classical analysis of the dramatic irony as an inadvertent foreshadowing, an un-self-comprehended prophecy, reveal the more central twisting of the ironic machine?) In the narrative realm, such instances abound in *Paradise Lost.* "Or when we lay," argues Belial, invoking recent pains (II, 168–69), "Chain'd on the burning Lake? that sure was worse," unaware that he is echoing the narrator's previous description of the nature of Satan's vastness: "So stretcht out huge in length the Arch-fiend lay / Chain'd on the burning Lake" (I, 209–10). The echo, which includes the enjambed "lay," is of a voice Belial has never heard, an epic narrator possessed of some "Foreknowledge absolute." The reader is reminded again how Belial is limited by his ignorance of the script written for him (once he has surrendered his freedom by choosing Satan and the fiction of self-createdness). Even as the modern reader hears a secondary echo, in this and other instances of repeated phrase throughout *Paradise Lost,* of the classical formulaic epithet, he implicitly surveys the distance between fallen angels such as Belial and the Homeric personages who are both his poetic forbears and, in the remodeled mythological history of *Paradise Lost,* his historical descendants.

In general, when Milton's poem echoes itself, whether from nearby or at a great distance, there is no ironic shift of voice, as in the previous case. In its wordplay, for example, *Paradise Lost* favors the echoing sort, rather than the compact form of the single word: *antanaclasis* rather than strict pun. In the rhetoric of wit, this is usually the weaker form (imagine, for example, "Now is the winter of our discontent / Made glorious summer by this sun of York's / Own son"), where the repetition has the plonking quality of self-glossing in the worst way. In many cases in Shakespeare's sonnets, or in lines like Donne's "When thou hast done, thou hast not done," the antanaclastic repetition embodies a compact pun (so that in order to gloss itself, the line would have to end "thou hast not done [Donne]," and it is only the second "done" which is being played upon). It is likely that the excessively unfunny antanaclasis with which Satan sneaks into Paradise, when "in contempt, / At one slight bound high overleap'd all bound / Of Hill or highest Wall" (IV, 181–82), is mimetically bad—even if Satan's leap is as graceful as that of the winner over the tennis net, the epic voice, in describing it, must change its notes to corny. At such close range, echoing repetition controls the ironies that inhere in the relation of the punning meanings, rather than those dramatic ironies that change of time and place will make literal.

More typical in *Paradise Lost* is the slightly deformed antanaclasis which Abraham Fraunce in *The Arcadian Rhetorike* (1588) reserved for the usual term *paranomasia* (which he also calls "allusion," interestingly enough, from the *ludus* of wordplay): thus Satan in Book I sneers at the benign rule of the King of Heaven (whom he has just accused of being *tyrannos* rather than *basileus* anyway), who "still his strength conceal'd, / Which tempted our attempt, and wrought our

fall" (I, 641–42). Milton has given Satan the advertent
wordplay here, as Adam is given the gentler and more lov-
ing wit, the beautiful and beautifully complex invocation to
Eve in Book IV (411): "Sole partner and sole part of all these
joys." (Here, as Alistair Fowler points out, the two meanings of *sole*—"only" and "unrivalled" are also at work.) But
love commands more intricate wit than hate does, and the
way in which we are reminded that *part* is part of *partner*—
an echo of stem rather than of suffix—is one worthy of
George Herbert.

Closely related to Belial's echo of the voice of the
narration—indeed, a kind of antitype of it—is Satan's echo
of an earlier formula in his speech on Mt. Niphates (IV,
42–45). At a strange moment of inadvertent admission of a
truth about his relation to God that he had previously (and
publicly) denied, he avers that

> he deserv'd no such return
> From me, whom he created when I was
> In that bright eminence, and with his good
> Upbraided none . . .

This is the Satan who, enthroned at the beginning of Book II
in a fierce but inauthentic splendor—its description may
itself echo Spenser's representation of the throne of Lucifera
(*Faerie Queene* I. iv. 8)—"exalted sat, by merit rais'd / To
that bad eminence" (II, 5–6). The memory of the "bright
eminence" echoes the reader's earlier apprehension of the
bad one, but the dramatic irony is softer here than it was in
the case of Belial. An even more poignant echo of the inex-
orable narrative voice occurs in Book IX, where Satan is at
one of his most moving moments in the poem.

He has just made his second mistake about Paradise. (The
first is in Book IV, 505–8, where he attributes to the unfallen
Adam and Eve, as they make love in a sight to him "hateful"
and "tormenting," the necessity for the consolations and

errors of fallen eroticism. He says of them that they were "Imparadis't in one another's arms / The happier Eden." Satan is wrong because they are "imparadis't" indeed in Paradise; the notion that an erotic embrace is a bower of bliss is a desperate, lovely fiction of fallen humanity.) A complementary mistake also results from Satan's being smitten with beauty in Paradise: addressing Earth (IX, 99ff), Satan praises the scene before him, feels the need of rhetorical elevation, then rationalizes the hyperbole: "O Earth, how like to Heav'n, if not preferr'd / More justly, Seat worthier of Gods, as built / With second thoughts, reforming what was old!" Then comes a second order of rationalization: Earth is better because it is the newer model, "For what God after better worse would build?" Again, *le pauvre,* Satan can only respond in fallen human terms of work, enterprise, and progress. It reciprocates for the mistake about love in Book IV. From the beauty of Earth and the nobility of its inhabitants ("Growth, Sense, Reason all summ'd up in Man"—a purely humanist notion), Satan moves to the deep pleasure yielded by landscape, pleasure unfallen yet, for humanity or for the seventeenth century, into the declensions of Beautiful, Picturesque, and Sublime, but summing them all up:

> If I could joy in aught, sweet interchange
> Of Hill and Valley, Rivers, Woods and Plains,
> Now Land, now Sea, and Shores with Forest crown'd,
> Rocks, Dens, and Caves; but I in none of these
> Find place or refuge . . .

(IX, 115–19)

"Rocks, Dens and Caves . . ." Satan finds no refuge in these, and particularly in the dialectic of array and design in pictures and spectacles of them. The reader will remember that the adventurous Drakes and Magellans of Pandemonium in Book II passed "O'er many a Frozen, many a Fiery Alp, /

Rocks, Caves, Lakes, Fens, Bogs, Dens, and shades of Death" (II, 620–21). That famous line of monosyllables over which the steps of prosodic theorists have for so long tripped is immediately echoed in the next line, "A Universe of death. . . ." Not only is Satan's longing catalogue of the joys of contemplated landscape bound to conclude in the places of retreat and darkness, prefiguring the meaning of shadiness that will eventually become attached to dark places after Adam and Eve first guiltily hide themselves there. He is, moreover, echoing the narration's understanding of the proleptically fallen relation, in Book II's prophetic vision of human culture, of rocks and dens and caves with death.

Adam's reflex of this kind of Satanic echoing—echoing of what has already, and in just those words, been propounded—can be heard in his patently rhetorical antanaclasis at IX, 1067. The first words he says to Eve after they awaken, "as from unrest," from their first fallen fucking in a "shady bank, / Thick overhead with verdant roof imbowr'd" (IX, 1037–38) are: "O Eve, in evil hour thou didst give ear / To that false Worm . . ." (IX, 1067–68). This is the same rhetorical Adam of the "sole partner and sole part," affirming the new fallen phenomenology of Eve's name: it no longer echoes "even," "eve," "evening," but now, as henceforth, "evil." In addition, he, like Satan, is echoing the narration. Less than three hundred lines before, Eve had stretched out her hand "in evil hour / Forth reaching to the Fruit" (IX, 780–81). Adam speaks almost with a tone of "indeed, Milton was right in saying that it was 'in evil hour' that this occurred," a tinct of wisdom never given to Satan. It is only the poetry of fallen man that will need to employ tropes and fables, similes, echoes, and allusions, in order to represent Truth. We somehow know that Adam is far less mocked by the dramatic irony of the narrative echo than Satan is, tortured ironist though he may be.

The chorus of echoes which accompanies the scenes of loss and regret surrounding the Fall is completed by the narration's own playback of an already resounding phrase. It occurs in the digression on the nature of the fig leaves with which human nakedness—the fallen form of nudity, ever to require *clothing,* as nudity itself, if concealed, is always to be veiled by visionary *drapery*—first hides itself ("Honor dishonorable!"). The fig tree is associated with a benign primitive role in a Rousseauian nature: the "Indian Herdsman shunning heat / Shelters in cool" (IX, 1108–9). It is this exotic tree, benevolent and protective in the more exotic and childlike of human cultures, that

> spreads her arms
> Branching so broad and long, that in the ground
> The bended Twigs take root, and Daughters grow
> About the Mother tree, a Pillar'd shade
> High overarch't, and echoing walks between.
>
> (IX, 1103–7)

Shade in Paradise is a lovely variation from sunlight; this "Pillar'd shade," and that of the "shady bank / Thick overhead with verdant roof imbowr'd" have already been imprinted with the shadowy type of death. In Book I, 301–3, the famous and heavily allusive image of the fallen legions of the rebel "Angel Forms" shows them as lying "Thick as autumnal Leaves that strow the Brooks / In Vallombrosa, where th' Etrurian shades / *High overarch't* imbower" (my italics). The specific verbal echo accompanies the shadows cast by the earlier text on the futurity of all shady places. And, as elsewhere in Milton, the rhetorical echo calls up the literal acoustical event: "echoing walks between."

There is something like a dramatic irony in a character's inadvertent echo of the narrative voice by which even his own utterance is recounted. There is also, as we have been seeing, a kind of allusive typology in the more possibly

self-aware echo of an earlier moment in Miltonic narration
by a later one. We might compare these two conditions with
the different kinds of irony revealed by the sense of unwitting literalness. In a phrase like Miranda's "O brave new
world . . . ," the audience recognizes an allusion to a literal
hemisphere, of which the speaker is ignorant. Much more
like Miltonic allusive irony is Abraham's remark to Isaac, in
response to the boy's question about what lamb will be used
for the sacrifice. "God will provide his own lamb," replies
the Kierkegaardian religious hero; the dramatic irony is
again generated by the unwitting literalness of what had
been propounded as a trope, here a trope of evasion. But the
Christian reading of this episode (not the *akeda* of the Hebrew Bible, but the first figurative sacrifice foreshadowing
the trope of Christ as lamb), gives the literalness another
dimension. What Abraham offers figuratively, the narrative
literalizes when the ram is discovered entangled in the
thicket. But the literalization is only a movement into the
fullness of antitype: the foreshadowing will be literally
fulfilled in the typological completion of the episode in the
New Testament when the Lamb of God is finally provided
by, and of, him.

It is this kind of dramatic and typological irony that is at
work in so many of those highly charged rhetorical moments in *Paradise Lost.* It lurks in the contortions of Satan's
manipulations of the literal and the figurative, the local and
the general ("Evil be thou my Good" completed by the
whining of "All good to me becomes / Bane" in Book IX,
for example). Indeed, we might learn from the shadows of
the unwitting in Satan's rhetoric, and in that of Adam when
he echoes Satan in syntax and tone (as in IX, 755–75), how
central to dramatic irony this question of inadvertent literalness can be. (Kafka's great parable *On Parables* also sheds
fierce light on this.) Dramatic irony is often a matter of an
utterance striking an unwitting *Vorklang,* as it were, of an

eventual echo, of a situation to which it will turn out to have alluded. It might be redefined in terms of manifest rhetorical figuration turning out, horribly, to have been literal. Certainly, Satanic rhetoric provides an origination of this.

One kind of self-echo in Milton occurs in the almost leitmotivic reappearance of phrases and cadences in *Paradise Lost* to which sophisticated critical attention of the past few decades has been so attentive. These form a subclass of their own. As echoes, their voices do not come from afar, or from absent places, so much as from a memory of the poem's own utterance. Their region of origin is usually schematically related to that of the echoic answer: thus, in Book V, the Son sits "Amidst as from a flaming Mount, whose top / Brightness had made invisible" (V, 598–99); the reversal of "No light, but rather darkness visible" (I, 63) points up the radically different character of the flaming. But such patterns are quite basic to the fabric of *Paradise Lost,* and might be considered as elements in what seems to be the poem's memory of itself.[9]

A most beautiful regathering of fragments of one's own text occurs in the lyrical last paragraph of Joyce's "The Dead," when two phrases uttered in innocence by Mary Jane earlier in the story—"snow was general all over Ireland" and, about monks sleeping in their coffins, "to remind them of their last end"—return with wider significance. In the final moment of the story, as the snow itself and Gabriel Conroy's journey "westward" all dissolve into allegory, the generalizing process is conjured up by echoes and by the

9. Like the deferred naming of the muse Urania, this whole pattern of self-echo in *Paradise Lost* probably derives from *The Faerie Queene*. Whether in the immediately repeating punning figures (e.g., Mercilla's sword, "Whose long rest rusted the bright steely brand") or the long-ranging memories (e.g., "Poore Colin Clout (who knowes not Colin Clout?)" of VI. 10. 16 and "Of Arlo-hill (Who knowes not Arlo-hill?)" of VII. 6. 36, Spenserian echoing is a most complex matter. Where, and why, this sort of thing happens in Spenser is worth studying.

beautiful *chiasmus* in the last sentence: "His soul swooned slowly as he heard the snow falling faintly through the universe and faintly falling, like the descent of their last end, upon all the living and the dead." This is much more like the Miltonic process in *Paradise Lost* than like devices Joyce would later develop (as, for example, the reversal of echo—fragment before whole utterance—in the operatic prologue to "Sirens" in *Ulysses,* and certainly in *Finnegans Wake*).

Among the informal schemes of echo there is the kind of repetition which suggests a flat or dead, rather than a hollow, rebound. A most obvious example of this is one in which a direct repetition most unexpectedly blocks out an expected antithesis or negation: "What is it men in women do require? / The lineaments of gratified desire. / What is it women do in men require? / The lineaments of gratified desire" (William Blake, "A Question Answered"—my punctuation). This is not only satire directed against sick views of the relations between the sexes, but against the very form of epigrammatic wit in which such views, masked as mature scepticism, would usually be embodied. The repetition demands, for its proper oral enunciation, a hint of the tone of "Sorry! you expected some clever reversal, appropriate to what you and I know to be the conflicting desires that make for the war between the sexes; but. . . ." It is not that the repetition is merely antiwitty (if wit be confined to the realm of the punch line), but that its mode of wit is allusive and dialectical, e.g., it is implicitly contrasting its own form with an unstated anterior one.

An example from the King James translation of the book of Proverbs (Chapter 26) should make this clearer:

> Answer not a fool according to his folly, lest thou
>   also be like unto him.
> Answer a fool according to his folly, lest he be wise
>   in his own conceit.

Each of these "parallel" verses gets its sharpness of point by contrast with the other. Perhaps most proverbs, if they have any force at all, are implicit exceptions taken to, or revisionary denials of, previous ones. "Absence makes the heart grow fonder" and "Out of sight is out of mind" are comically juxtaposed as if to show thereby the moral emptiness of proverbial formulation—they cannot both be true, and therefore neither must be able to be. But if either one is read with the contrasting one as an implicit epigraph (viz., "You might have heard that 'Absence . . . etc.,' but, in fact, out of sight is out of mind"), the rhetorical force of antithetical, systematic, nay-*but*-saying is added. I think that most proverb literature works in this way, and that there is an implicit moral commonplace being denied even in the official wisdom which Blake's proverbs—or Oscar Wilde's, or Shaw's, or Samuel Butler's—so explicitly revise.

The implicit contrastive mode is somehow at work in those echoing figures, like certain kinds of refrain, which seem to have the otherwise inexplicable force of "R *but* R," logically improper but rhetorically possible. These are like counter-echoes, mocking resoundings of an original voice not heard.

One observation might be added here about echoes that are difficult to recognize as such, not so much because the original voice is absent, but because voice and echo are so close together as to be indistinguishable. We saw earlier that a certain amount of echoing overhang is necessary in every actual human acoustical situation in order to avoid a sense of sonic death, of an absorbent ambiance that gobbles up all the morsels of speech or song we produce, returning none and thus ruining our full perception of what we ourselves utter. The analogy hardly holds for textual echoes. But a peculiar instance of an intense echo seeming to resound within a word itself can be identified in those private resonances of a particular word that have so concerned the modern imagination. These might include a Hopkinsian revelation of the "inscape" of a particular word, or the young Joycean narrator's immersion in the self-echoing word "paralysis"— which, indeed, reechoes thematically through the whole of *Dubliners* (and even in Joyce's well-known statement about the book, in a letter later on, invoking Dublin as the "center of its [Ireland's] paralysis"). Anyone who has ever had even a momentary or ad hoc mantra—whether so named or dignified by Oriental fad or not—may want to consider the concept of a word which seems to echo itself.

Perhaps the most celebrated poetic instance of a purely self-echoing situation—albeit of a totally different sort— might be the way of rhyming that admits only repetition of the word itself, in a particular case. The *terza rima* of *The Divine Comedy,* that scheme which is quintessentially repetitive and generative at once, amplifies in each tercet the echoing rhyme of the minor, middle line of the preceding one. But in *Paradiso* XXXII, interlocking with the rhyme word *Cristo* in the previous tercet, comes an astonishingly significant flatness:

> Riguarda omai nella faccia ch'a Cristo
>   più si somiglia, chè la sua chiarezza
>   sola ti può disporre a veder Cristo
>
> (Look now at the face most like Christ;
> for only its brightness can fit you
> to see Christ)   (XXXII, 85–87)

The word, naming perfection, can rhyme with no other. It resounds, in a very different way from previous instances, only with, and in, itself.

A further refinement of this scheme might be the reanimation of the otherwise dead, or redundant, echo by ironic elicitation of a latent meaning—rather like the traditional device of wit which enlivens a cliché or dead metaphor. A splendid instance is, of course, the narrator's answer to the anguished cry of the unlucky Fortunato in Poe's "The Cask of Amontillado," on discovering that he is indeed being walled up alive: "'*For the love of God, Montresor!*' 'Yes,' I said, 'for the love of God.'" Or Stephen Dedalus' answer to Ghezzi in *A Portrait of the Artist,* when he is told that Bruno was "a terrible heretic": "'he was terribly burned.'"

The apparent echoing of solitary words is a subject about which there is much to say, and I merely wish to introduce it here. It does remind us, however, that acoustical echoing in empty places can be a very common auditory emblem, redolent of gothic novels as it may be, of isolation and often of unwilling solitude. This is no doubt a case of natural echoes conforming to echo's mythographic mocking, rather than affirming, role. In an empty hall that should be comfortably inhabited, echoes of our voices and motions mock our very presence in the hollow space. One outstanding poetic instance of the total reversal of this echo of affright is one of the most beautiful and celebrated treatments of allegorical echo in our language. In Milton's *Comus,* the Lady lost in the wood cries out to her brothers, hoping that "such noise as I can make" will be heard by them. Instead of merely shouting, or even praying for greater amplification of her voice, she sings—this being a masque, in which song initiates transformations—her famous song to Echo, asking the nymph to tell her where her brothers are. I shall return to the song shortly. In the lines closely—but not directly—preceding the song, there occurs a most significant example of the flat or dead self-echo we have previously considered. The Lady has been encountering phantasms in her memory, but then expunges them with thoughts ("I see ye visibly") of Faith, Hope, and, the greatest of these (for the fifteen-year-old Alice Egerton who was playing the part of, and whose psyche *was,* the Lady), Chastity. She can believe that a "glist'ring Guardian" might be sent her, "To keep my life and honor unassail'd." And then,

> Was I deceiv'd, or did a sable cloud
> Turn forth her silver lining on the night?
> I did not err, there does a sable cloud
> Turn forth her silver lining on the night,
> And casts a gleam over this tufted Grove.
>   (lines 221–24)

It is hard to imagine these lines read aloud, whether or not they were to be performed with some stage effect. Indeed, the deadly strict repetition seems almost a cliché of parody of amateur theatricals, smacking of Pyramus and Thisbe. But it is important that these lines were never uttered by Alice Egerton in the Masque Presented at Ludlow Castle in 1634. They were added later on for a printed text only. Scholarly conjecture that Milton may have been using a pattern he knew from an Ovidian text seems quite plausible. In the *Fasti* (V, 549), with respect to why, in May, the radiant sun rises more quickly, Ovid interjects: "fallor, an arma sonant? non fallimur, arma sonabant" ("am I wrong, or did arms ring out? I'm not wrong, arms rang out"). Mars comes, and he and his temple are invoked. Milton may certainly have adopted the pattern in these textual—rather than vocable—lines. Perhaps he was thinking also of the rising light, and the—for him—menacing figure of Mars as a prefiguration of the arrival of Comus in response to the music, but not the words, of the song to Echo. In any event, Milton added this dead echo as the summation and conclusion of a conceptually and doctrinally crucial passage designed to precede the Echo song. It is as if, the performance itself perhaps echoing in his head, he were affirming his own relation to the regions—caves, cells, whatever—sacred to Echo herself. Whether he added it as a scheme of echoing like the ones we have been exploring, or whether it was accompanied merely by an ad hoc sense of how this repetition was rather like an echo, the lines triumph, with the victory of significance, over the clumsiness of the repetition.

The song itself can hardly be considered an example of echo song, or even to include any element of schematic textual echo:

> Sweet Echo, sweetest Nymph that liv'st unseen
>> Within thy airy shell
> By slow *Meander*'s margent green,
> And in the violet-embroider'd vale
>   Where the love-lorn Nightingale
> Nightly to thee her sad Song mourneth well.
>
> Canst thou not tell me of a gentle Pair
>> That likest thy *Narcissus* are?
>>> O if thou have
>> Hid them in some flow'ry Cave,
>>> Tell me but where,
> Sweet Queen of Parley, Daughter of the Sphere,
> So mayst thou be translated to the skies,
> And give resounding grace to all Heav'n's Harmonies.

These lines have been discussed in great detail by Milton scholars,[10] and I would only call attention here to a few points. First, the matter of *location* is important: where Echo dwells is a major matter, and the transformation of her "cell" in the acting version of the masque, to "shell" in Milton's signed published text, has all sorts of resonances. Most important of all, however, may be that this song occurs in deliberate lieu of a formal echo song. Comus' mother, Circe, called up echoes as broadcasting devices in William Browne's *Inner Temple Masque* (1614), in order to assemble a congress of all the nymphs:

10. See *A Variorum Commentary on the Poems of John Milton,* ed. M. Y. Hughes et al. (New York, 1972) II, 891–95; also, Angus Fletcher, *The Transcendental Masque* (Ithaca and London, 1971), 198–209.

For powerful Circe; and let in a song
Echoes be aiding, that they may prolong
My now command to each place where they be,
To bring them hither all more speedily.

*Presently in the wood was heard a full music of lutes which, descending to
the stage, had to them sung this following song, the Echoes being placed in
several parts of the boscage.*

    Song of the Nymphs in the wood
Circe bids you come away,
  Echo. Come away, come away.
From the rivers, from the sea,
  Echo. From the sea, from the sea.
From the green woods every one,
  Echo. Every one, every one.
Of her maids be missing none,
  Echo. Missing none, missing none.
No longer stay except it be to bring
 A med'cine for love's sting;
That would excuse you and be held more dear
Than wit or magic, for both they are here.
 Echo. They are here, they are here.

The phrase "come away," an early seventeenth-century
lyric cliché, also served to introduce an echo song in Ben
Jonson's 1605–6 *Masque of Blackness*. Jonson had introduced
the figure of Echo herself in *Cynthia's Revels,* where the
whole scene is remarkable for its sophisticated array of echo
devices in the schematic surface, and for the way in which
the mythography of Echo is deepened (as we saw above, in
chapter 2). In the play, Mercury invokes the nymph herself:

Salute me with thy repercussive voice,
That I may know that caverne of the earth
Contains thy ayrie spirit, how, or where
I may direct my speech, that thou maist heare.

—to which Echo, as she appears for the first time, responds
with two deft and resonant puns. "Here" she echoes; then

Mercury: "So nigh?" and again, "I." When "hear" is here and "I" (as well as "aye!") is nigh, Echo is present. In the ensuing dialogue, Echo responds not with fragmentary re-sounding, but with the rhetorical figure of anadiplosis, taking up Mercury's last word. Her song ("Slow, slow, fresh fount, keepe time with my salt teares") starts out with the rhyme of Mercury's last couplet. Its first line calls up the refrain of Spenser's "Prothalamion": "Sweete Thames, runne softly till I end my song," itself a line to resound for ages.

The Lady's song to Echo in *Comus* is perhaps a kind of answer to Jonson's, ending, similarly, with an alexandrine. It is also a replacement, a kind of allusive substitution for, the song in such masques as Browne's and Jonson's (both *Blackness* and *Beauty*). The relation of the nymph to water (the scene originates the Fountain of Self-Love in Jonson's fable) is recapitulated in *Comus* with the eventual appearance of the river nymph Sabrina, who does indeed sing in response to the song which calls her up.

The power of Milton's mythmaking here extends beyond the text of *Comus* itself. Charles Brockden Brown's demonic, failed poet, Carwin the "biloquist" (in *Wieland*), tells us in a fragmentary memoir published in 1822 of how he became a ventriloquist. Encountering an extraordinary array of echoes in a mountain glen ("The spot where I stood was buried in dusk, but the eminences were still invested with a luminous and vivid twilight"), he becomes enchanted by their variety. He returns to his "vocal glen," and "thence scrambling up a neighbouring steep, which overlooked a wide extent of this romantic country, gave myself up to contemplation, and the perusal of Milton's *Comus*." In the subsequent paragraphs, in which the wretched Carwin resolves to learn to dispose his organs of speech so as to make his voice appear at a distance, there is no more mention of the Miltonic source. But it is clear that *Comus'* fable of Echo is being revised into a later fiction of artificial echo as ventriloquism, and as poetry of a kind.

The *Comus* song, then, deepens and transforms the mythical personification of Echo, not only by being aware of earlier versions of her and attempting to move through and beyond these. It does so in an aria which moves beyond the mechanics of the echo song.[11] Whether derisive in its fragmentary return, affirming in its pastoral authentications, or exudingly lyrical in a baroque form of choral recapitulation, these schemes all embody patterns of repeating oneself. It is as if in *Comus* Milton had deliberately eschewed what would have been an easy, and familiar, effect, and had instead internalized textual echoing in the song itself. His modes of self-echo in *Paradise Lost* and *Samson Agonistes* would be of a very different sort, rebounds across great distances of text and mythological phase.

The echo device and its variant schemes of refrain and patterned repetition can have, as we have seen, a force of figuration much deeper than that of mere decorative patterning. In the very rhetoric of returning only part of an utterance, there is something of trope always implicit, just as one or another of the mythologies of the Nymph herself—mocking, lamenting, assenting, amplifying, and, indeed, interpreting—can always be adduced.[12] I should like to conclude this section, and introduce the next one, by returning for a moment to the original Ovidian scene. Here is George Sandys' version (1621) of Ovid's "dixerat: 'ecquis

11. Such as, for example, the scene in George Peele's *The Old Wives' Tale,* in which two brothers, searching for an endangered sister, are counseled by Echo. Milton's scene "replaces" this one—it is as if the Lady in *Comus* were recalling Peele, implicitly saying, "Sweet Echo, who helped Delya's brothers find *her* in the old play. . . ."

12. I realize that this touches on matters of contemporary rhetorical theory, and on competing views, structuralist and otherwise, on the relation of metonymy and synecdoche, the representation of wholes by parts, and so forth, which I shall not discuss here.

adest?' et 'adest' responderat Echo" ([he] said: "Is anyone here?" and "Here" Echo answered):

> The Boy, from his companions parted, said;
> Is any nigh? I, *Eccho* answer made.

Very nicely done. And yet—as we may or may not remember—the same response, with the same pun (I/aye), is made to Mercury by Ben Jonson's Echo in *Cynthia's Revels,* some two decades earlier. To come across it in Sandys is indeed like hearing a repetition or echo across a great distance. It reminds us of the central metaphoric use of our word, which ordinarily names an acoustical phenomenon in honor of the departed nymph, to mean an allusive resounding, a rebound across a gap not merely of many lines of text, but of many texts as well. Sandys "echoes" Jonson, *in* an echo device, *about* the poignancy of the fragmentation of utterance when it is rebounded. In Jonson's case, Mercury and ourselves are awakened to the *aye, I* implicit in *nigh* whenever the nymph is asked if she is present. Echo song about Echo is an easy instance of imitative form, but Sandys' echoing of Jonson may not be so trivial a borrowing as it seems. He uses the most pregnant and resonant response in Jonson's whole scene, and he implicitly refers back to the context of its occurrence: Mercury addresses Echo to find out "what caverne of the earth / Contains thy ayrie spirit"— that crucial request for location of the disembodied voice that, wherever it is, occupies no space. Echo is voice's self,[13] and Sandys, sensible of all this, brings back the later consequences of the Ovidian mythmaking in translating the origination. This is an early analogue of Pope's echoing Tasso and Milton in translating Homer. It leads us to consider this mode of "echo" now in greater detail.

13. Yeats' late poem, "The Man and the Echo," affirms this. The "Rocky Voice" which plays no verbal tricks in its answers comes at the end of the tradition of the echo scheme. Its irony is that it is not expectedly ironic.

IV.
Echo Metaphorical

Everything we hear is an echo. Anyone can see that echoes move forward and backward in time, in rings. But not everyone realizes that as a result silence becomes harder and harder for us to grasp—though in itself it is unchanged—because of the echoes pouring through us out of the past, unless we can learn to set them at rest. We are still hearing the bolting of the doors of Hell, Pasiphae in her byre, the cries at Thermopylae, and do not recognize the sounds. How did we sound to the past? And there are sounds that rush away from us: echoes of future words.

So we know that there are words in the future, some of them loud and terrible. And we know that there is silence in the future. But will the words recognize their unchanging homeland? . . .

W. S. MERWIN

When we speak metaphorically of echoes between texts, we imply a correspondence between a precursor and, in the acoustical actuality, a vocal source. What is interesting and peculiar about this is that whereas in nature, the anterior source has a stronger presence and authenticity, the figurative echoes of allusion arise from the later, present text. But it has many sorts of priority over what has been recalled in it. In one way, the relation of echo and source is like the curious dialectic of "true" meanings of words: the etymon and the present common usage each can claim a different kind of authority. (The dialectic might be called the field of combat between synchrony and diachrony. That field is the domain of poetry as well.)

We also imply that the fragment of present utterance, the mite of quotation which is unquoted (by conscious or unwitting design), has been broken off from the context of a more complete utterance, as well as a prior one. It is, of course, incorporated into a new utterance. Let us put this element back into a natural metaphor. In order to hear, across a valley, the equivalent of an allusive echo, our call of "Hello" should have to resound not merely as "Hello" (or a series of "Hello"'s, or even "—lo," or a series of those), but rather as, say, "Lo! the hills answer," or "Low, low, low, our voices slowly fall," or even "Hello is hollow." Consider, on the other hand, these possibilities: "And 'Hello' to you, too," or "'Hello' is right," or "Attention please, echo coming: 'Hello,'" or "As you so recently put it, 'Hello.'" We should have to call a voice of valley or cave that sent back such a response a natural allusion, or quotation, rather than an echo. The distinction seems to be drawn with respect to the degree, and kind, of incorporation of the vocal source in the response, and to the subtlety and profundity of the mode of response itself.

It will also be noticed that both of these matters tend to elicit, at least in these examples, punning, or something very like it—some play on or with the words of the vocal source. The Latin rhetorical term for such word play is *allusio,* and it is useful to remember that punning is, in our modern sense, allusive, or even echolike, to the degree that it alludes to—or invokes or calls up or quotes—other "meanings." (And if we momentarily treat a "meaning" as the voice of an intention, the echo analogy fits even better.) We might even, in fact, go so far as to be able to distinguish "good" from "bad" puns by observing whether they were more like echoes, allusions, or blatant quotations. That is, we would evaluate the incorporation of an alluded-to meaning in the utterance that frames the primary one, the subtlety and profundity of the relation between the two and, of course, the degree of distortion—verbal and syntactical—in the adaptation of one word to another.

We might, indeed, propose a kind of rhetorical hierarchy for the relationship of allusive modes. Actual *quotation,* the literal presence of a body of text, is represented or replaced by *allusion,* which may be fragmentary or periphrastic. In the case of outright allusion, as Reuben Brower pointed out so well in his *Alexander Pope: The Poetry of Allusion,* the text alluded to is not totally absent, but is part of the portable library shared by the author and his ideal audience. Intention to allude recognizably is essential to the concept, I think, and that concept is circumscribed genetically by earlier sixteenth-century uses of the word *alluding* that are closer to the etymon *ludus*—the senses of "punning" and "troping." Again it should be stated that one cannot in this sense allude unintentionally—an inadvertent allusion is a kind of solecism.[1]

But then there is echo, which represents or substitutes for allusion as allusion does for quotation. There seems to be a transitive figurational connection among them; it points to what we generally mean by *echo,* in intertextual terms. In contrast with literary allusion, echo is a metaphor of, and for, alluding, and does not depend on conscious intention. The referential nature of poetic echo, as of dreaming (or Coleridgean "symbol" as opposed to conscious "allegory"), may be unconscious or inadvertent, but is no less qualified thereby. In either case, a pointing to, or figuration of, a text recognized by the audience is not the point.

Take, for example, the famous lyric from William Carlos Williams' *Spring and All* (1923), "By the road to the contagious hospital." The second line—which enjambs so remarkably into the third ("under the surge of the blue/ mottled clouds driven from the northeast")—has two readings. The first, or end-stopped one, suggests that

1. Quintilian (*Institutes* I. v. 53) observes this of figuration generally; for him, an unintentional metaphor is a blunder.

"blue" is a substantive, a synecdoche for "sky" as well as Blueness. The second, discovered when we read into the next line, reveals "blue" to be adjectival, and part of the ugly deadly mottling. But the hopefulness of "the surge of the blue" will in fact be redeemed in the course of the poem. Now, the "cold wind," at first taken as one more sign of continued winter, is revealed, as "one by one objects are defined," to be the wind of spring; the buds that looked like death turn out to be germs of life; and the destroyed to be in fact the preserved. Shelley's west wind, the "destroyer and preserver both," comes with "the locks of the approaching storm," "Spread/On the blue surface of thine aery surge." There might be no reason to assume that an aggressively modernist poem like this one might have re-collected the "blue" and "surge" in such a way—it is Keats, in any event, who haunted Williams' earliest poems—were it not for the locality of theme from which the earlier voice rebounds. A seasonal wind of change whose meaning must be interpreted blows through each poem, and while Shelley's mode of revelation is prophetic, and Williams' almost epistemological, the great epiphany of process is engendered in both cases.

The reader of texts, in order to overhear echoes, must have some kind of access to an earlier voice, and to its cave of resonant signification, analogous to that of the author of the later text.[2] When such access is lost in a community of reading, what may have been an allusion may fade in prominence; and yet a scholarly recovery of the context would restore the allusion, by revealing an intent as well as by

2. I. A. Richards, in *The Principles of Literary Criticism* (London, 1929), 215–19), warns against too great a sensitivity to allusion on the part of the critic. But he makes no distinction between manifest allusion or quotation and problematically overt echo; and in any case, it was his pointing out the echo of Tennyson in Empson's villanelle (discussed later in chapter 4) that, years ago, helped lead me to my present concern.

showing means. In the case of some allusions in the implicit
contrastive mode discussed earlier, the loss of textual background seems more to result in something like echo. Thus,
"Fourscore and seven years ago, our fathers brought forth
on this continent a new nation, conceived in liberty . . ." is
seldom considered an allusive text—indeed, it has been
claimed by American folklore as the opening of a monu-
ment of the antimonumental, of noble plain style, balanced,
yet schematically sinewy. But the implicit contrasts set up a
powerful pair of tropes, and either lack of appropriate access
to scripture or exigetical *pudeur* has passed them over. They
might be sketched out as follows: (1) "*Whereas in the beginning, at Our Father's command, the earth brought forth grass . . .*
(Genesis 1:12), a mere fourscore and seven years ago our
forefathers brought forth on this piece of earth a new nation" and (2) "Whereas man is *conceived in* sin, this nation
was conceived in liberty." The rhythm of "fourscore . . .
forth" makes us notice the ellipsis of "fore(—fathers)," but
that ellipsis itself makes the forebears into secular forms of
pater noster. Thus the two tropes make the new, but now no
longer young, nation into a natural, unfallen, new-Adamic
being. In the Gettysburg Address, even the word *nation* is
accompanied by biblical resonances.[3]

Even in patently allusive contexts, echoes of a more covert sort can lurk. Virgil's tenth eclogue is full of allusions to,
and paraphrases of, Theocritus' first idyll. Apollo's question
in lines 21–22—"What madness is this, Gallus? Your darling
Lycoris has followed another through snows and through
army camps bristling with war"—paraphrases a question
asked of Daphnis by Priapus in Theocritus I, 82–83. But the
final word of Theocritus' line, *kôra* (girl) is punningly
echoed and reechoed by the final cadence of Virgil's line:

3. Perhaps the canceled words, *upon the this continent,* in the first draft of
the Gettysburg Address indicate Lincoln's awareness of the biblical idiom.

"tua cura Lycoris" ("your darling, Lycoris"). The sequence *kôra—cura—Lycoris* also implicitly launders all traces of the root "wolf" from the girl's name, implying instead a poetic "etymology" from "girl" and "dear, cared for." Moreover, it absorbs, interprets, and returns the voice of Virgil's precursor Theocritus in a mode more personal than that of the public allusiveness of adaptation, imitation, and paraphrase.

At the end of the "Ode on the Morning of Christ's Nativity," Milton underscores the allusively Spenserian use, throughout, of the strophically terminal alexandrine, by a particular echo. In the description of the "courtly stable" where "bright-harnest Angels sit in order serviceable," the sound that returns is that of a line in *The Faerie Queene* Book VI (x.13), in Calidore's vision of Mt. Acidale. In a simile connecting the concentric rings of dancing girls and graces surrounding Colin Clout's Rosalind with the constellation Corona, Spenser says of the latter that it is "unto the starres an ornament / Which round about her move in order excellent." The "order serviceable" is a new angelic order occasioned by the desublimation of the godhead installed in the rustic baby. The particular Miltonic half-line of inversion, with its altered adjective, is hardly allusive. But it resonates in the cave or rocks of context—the figurative stellar coronation of a momentarily earthly spot, embraced in a moment of vision.

This echo is faint, and perhaps audible only to the well-tuned ear of a Keats, for example, who himself strikes echoes from Milton's *Ode*. It has often been noted that the "No shrine, no grove, no oracle, no heat / Of pale-mouthed prophet dreaming" of the "Ode to Psyche" calls up Milton's "No nightly trance, or breathèd spell / Inspires the pale-ey'd Priest from the prophetic cell." The voice of the line, with its echoic overlapping of elements, resounds as always in the chamber of context—not only among stanzas XIX and XX of Milton's *Ode,* but in that poem's very mode, superficially

unacknowledged, of making the newly unseated pagan mythology available for modern poetry. In a sense, Christ's
coming, which has desanctified such beings as Hercules,
permits that ancient hero to be used for the covert allusion,
at the end of the poem, of the infant strangling in his swad-
dling bands the whole suspect crew of false mysteries.
Keats' "Ode to Psyche" itself has a poetic function analogous to Milton's, for Keats, too (he jokes in a letter that he is
"far more orthodox than to let a pagan goddess go
neglected"), is reconsecrating mythology for poetry, and
here, specifically, a myth too late-born to seem central otherwise. And Keats, too, asks his Muse to "prevent" with his
humble ode the canonical judgment of history, as Milton
prays that his figurative orient gift be delivered before the
merely opulent spices of the magi.

Milton provides other resonant conformations of
ambiance—the ambiguously erotic quality of the descent of
"meek-eyed" Peace; the lines from stanza XX: "From
haunted spring, and dale/Edg'd with poplar pale"; perhaps
even the famous "blind mouths" of *Lycidas* as a resonant
paradigm of eye-mouth substitution. From all of these
chambers are gathered some of the "unnumbered sounds"
that were stored up in Keats' evening ear and which, he said,
"distance of recognizance bereaves" ("bereaves" in the literal sense of "fetching from afar," or carrying off from a
prior scene). The line about the "pale-mouth'd prophet"
echoes, rather than alludes. As with Milton and Spenser,
there is no reliance on the reader's possession of the text
referred to—it is almost as if the echo would appeal, not to
the audience for an allusion, but to the surrounding poem
itself. And as with dreams, which assemble fragments of
shadow and echo, the workings of this substitute for allusion may be unconscious. Whether they are or are not seems
less the point than that they are not overt allusions.

There are instances in *Paradise Lost,* for example, of an echo and allusion operating on the same material, and it might be instructive to look at one of them. In this case, the echo anticipates the direct allusion, perhaps as a Miltonic version of the pattern of deferred naming in *The Faerie Queene.* I am thinking of an echo of Ovid (*Metamorphoses* XIV, 628–30) in Book IX of *Paradise Lost:* Eve is likened to a wood-nymph, then to Artemis herself (line 389). Then we have the usual trope of qualification of the classical comparison: she is not armed, like Delia, with bow and quiver,

> But with such Gard'ning Tools as Art yet rude
> Guiltless of fire had form'd, or Angels brought.
> To Pales, or Pomona, thus adorn'd,
> Likest she seem'd, *Pomona* when she fled
> Vertumnus . . . (IX, 390–94)

Milton figuratively follows Ovid, in moving from Diana armed to Pomona, however pretechnologically equipped: Pomona herself (I give George Sandys' translation), "Her hand a hooke, and not a javelin bare: / Now prunes luxurious twigs, and boughes that dare / Transcend their bounds . . . " Readers who know Book IX well may hear some faint reverberation at this point. They need only turn back to lines 208ff. Adam is counseling Eve about the necessity—even in Paradise, where unfallen nature needs no agriculture—for that prelapsarian trope of husbandry, *gardening:* "The work under our labor," he says, "Grows / Luxurious by restraint; what we by day / Lop overgrown, or prune, or prop, or bind, / One night or two with wanton growth derides / Tending to wild . . . " Almost two hundred lines before the explicit (if complex) introduction of an allusive comparison of Eve to Pomona, Ovid's lines 629–30 (quoted in Sandys' translation above) are clearly echoed: Pomona carries the *falce,* or pruning hook, "qua mode luxuriem premit et spatiantia passim / bracchia conpescit" ("with which she now restrained the luxuriant growth and cut back the branches spreading everywhere"). The turning of the phrase to incorporate the dialectic of pruning ("less in order that more") by no means obliterates the resonance. Eve-as-Pomona has already been introduced before she is allusively named.

When we do in fact come to that naming, the connections with the Ovidian text have already been established. Thus the final linking of Pomona with Vertumnus, the god of seasonal and, more generally, metamorphic change, is a revisionary one. In Ovid's story, Vertumnus went through a Protean series of metamorphoses—itself as secondary and allusive to Jupiter's as Eve's nature is to Pomona's—in which he became a plowman, a dresser of vines, a "painefull Reaper," and a wintry old crone, by turns, in order to seduce Pomona. Sandys' mythographic commentary, like many others, interprets Vertumnus as the changing year, and adds that he is also "the inconstant mutability of our human affections." Milton has us read him as the arch-imager of Eve's garden, who needs only one change into crooked shape to win Eve and bring about a fallen natural world of seasonal rotation. Whether we characterize this shadowing of Satan as leaped over, implied, or suppressed—as three different rhetorical theories might do—it is, once again, the cave and rocks of the prior text whose shapes are called up by the echoed sounds in the later one.

Passages showing echo patterns, or invoking the affirmative echo mythology of pastoral, can be resonant in this allusive way as well. "The woods shall to me answer, and their eccho ring": Spenser's famous "Epithalamion" refrain (itself a private redoubling, perhaps, of "That all the woods with doubled eccho ring" of *Faerie Queene* I. vi. 14) becomes a source of later allusion. It is so insistent as to command the strophic closure in epithalamia by Donne, Jonson, and others in later decades. In Jonson's case, the

"Epithalamion: Or, a Song," for the marriage of Jerome Weston and Lady Frances Stuart in 1632, seems strongly conscious of Spenser's poem as a prototype. There are exactly twenty-four stanzas, and the opening lines—"Though thou has past thy summer standing, stay / Awhile with us, bright sun, and help our light"—hark back to another poem of marriage exactly at midsummer almost forty years earlier. (The antiphonal nature of echo within the line of Spenser's refrain seems to carry over to Jonson's poem as well.) In the following lines from it, it is hard not to hear the antiphonal bells as echoing yet another text:

> Hark, how the bells upon the waters play
> > Their sister-tunes, from Thames his either side,
> As they had learned new changes for the day,
> > As all did ring the approaches of the bride . . .

The two sides of the Thames might be Spenser's "Prothalamion" and Jonson's own poem; the echoing of the former in these four lines, and in other places in the poem, is haunting.

Spenser's echo of Virgilian echoing itself resounds in later poetry. In the celebrated refrain of the "Prothalamion," there is an ellipsis of what is almost echoing in that line which has been far better manifestly remembered than the rest of the poem—"Sweet Thames, runne softly till I end my song" (as if "And then you may echo and affirm its truth" were to follow).[4] T. S. Eliot's manifestly ironic completion of the "Prothalamion" refrain in *The Waste Land* has a strange, perhaps inadvertent, rightness—"Sweet Thames run softly for I speak not loud or long" is an alexandrine resonant of the major Spenserian closures of the other

4. Following Donald Cheney and others, I observe the punning overtone of "Sweet Time" in Spenser's refrain. It is possible that Denham, in his famous lines addressed to the Thames in *Cooper's Hill*—"O could I flow like thee, and make thy stream / My great example, as it is my theme!"— heard "Sweet Theme, runne softly" there as well.

poem: Spenser's own spousal verse turned out to have been
prophetic of his own death (for which Essex, himself to fall
two years later, would pay the funeral expenses). Eliot's
addition interprets the Thames refrain as applying to all
poetry and the death it momentarily holds at bay. It is echoic
in two ways. It employs that simplest rhetorical form of the
representation of echo, the repeated phrase, and it includes a
more ghostly, formal allusion to a whole Spenserian milieu
in its very metrical form. It is as if a mocking echo (Eliot's
manifest intention) were being accompanied by a quieter,
richer one. We hear an echo that affirms by interpreting a
prior textual voice.

Echo, allusion, and quotation, then, are forms of citation
that are clearly related and clearly distinct. We generally
bracket them under the heading of allusiveness, various aspects of which have concerned modern literary history and
interpretation from the start. In the past century, allusiveness has been studied in various ways: as *Quellenforschungen,*
as if the sources of the poetic Nile were not themselves
eloquent and derivative rivers; or as props to the infirmities
of unoriginality; or as one of a set of credentials, like water-
marks on paper, of the creative presence of an informed
will. The influence of literary modernism on academic research gave allusiveness another kind of credential power. It
became in Eliot, in Pound, and in the way in which they in
turn read Joyce, a mode of ironic distancing from the romanticism they spurned and craved. Indeed, the tendency
of modernism was almost to claim this ironic mode of allusiveness as purely its own. Harold Rosenberg, in a little
book on Arshile Gorky, makes this plain.[5]

5. Harold Rosenberg, *Arshile Gorky* (New York, 1962), 53–64. Of particular interest are his remarks on allusion, parody, and quotation, the first
of these being "the most profound, the true ghostly principle of historical
revival, since by allusion the thing alluded to is both there and not there."
(55–56).

But for readers of English and American poetry from *The Shepheardes Calender* to the present, the various engines of allusion have always been central to the poetic record and the poetic procedure. The way in which poets like Spenser, Jonson, Milton, and Marvell deal with prior texts seems a matter almost as important as the nature of poetic rhetoric (indeed, I shall suggest that it may be part of it). Prior forms, genres, and topoi occupied a public domain long before there were copyright laws, but the poetic infringement on personal rights through direct or inherent quotation is an important practice. What a great writer does with direct citation of another's language is quite different from what a minor one may be doing. Similarly, his handling of a commonplace will be radically interpretive of it, while the minor writer's contribution will be more one of handing on the baton, so to speak, of cultivating the topos rather than replanting or even building there. Sir Richard Fanshawe, for example, translating the famous passage about the Golden Age from Guarini's *Il Pastor Fido,* handles Guarini's allusion to prior writers—Tasso, Boethius, Ovid, Catullus, Horace—by quoting, without acknowledgment, Jonson's adaptation of Catullus: "Nor thinkest it any fault love's sweets to steal / So from the world thou canst the theft conceal" (a reversal of "Tis no sin love's fruit to steal, / But the sweet theft to reveal: / To be taken, to be seen," etc., from "To Celia"). He also reflects Samuel Daniel's version of Tasso's chorus from *Aminta:*

> Let's love! The sun doth set and rise again,
> But whenas our short light
> Comes once to set, it makes eternal night.

Fanshawe's concluding lines to his translation of Guarini echo this as: "Let's hope, the sun that's set may rise, / And with new light salute our longing eyes."[6]

6. Guarini's *Coro* on the Golden Age is so continuously attentive to its precursor passage in Tasso's *Aminta* that it is a virtual line-by-line parody.

These allusive schemes have the role of minor scholia, commenting on the relations among all the authorities on the subject in question, transported from the margin into the text. But we should have to consider in another way the echo, in the semichorus near the end of *Samson Agonistes,* in the famous passage about the phoenix,

> Like that self-begotten bird
> In the Arabian weeds embost
> That no second knows, nor third

where Shakespeare's cadences march through the lines in a kind of ghostly way. The momentarily headless tetrameters, the grammar of Shakespeare's "That defunctive music can," the modified "On the sole Arabian tree," almost make us want to search our text of "The Phoenix and Turtle" for the exact prototype of the line "That no second knows, nor Third." But the echoes of several lines, fragmented as echoes are, have perfectly blended. This is not a matter of mythographic footnotes on the phoenix of the sort we might find in the printed texts of Jonson's masques. In the very suppression of specific quotation, or direct allusion, this echo is rather like a trope as compared to Fanshawe's scheme.

Gilbert West, in his translation of the first Pythian ode of Pindar (London, 1749), writes in what Reuben Brower once characterized as "the just classical vein of Gray's 'Elegy.'"[7] The passage Brower quotes contrasts, with the sweet music of the fame of Croesus praised in the ode, the figurative cacophony of the bad name of the tyrant Phalaris, of whom West's Pindar says:

> Him therefore nor in sweet Society
>   The gen'rous Youth conversing ever name;

7. Reuben A. Brower, *Mirror on Mirror* (Cambridge, Mass., 1974), 51. My debt to this author's *Alexander Pope: The Poetry of Allusion* (Oxford, 1959) is great.

> Nor with the Harp's delightful Melody
> Mingle his odious inharmonious Fame.

The posthumous music denied the bad ruler is specifically that of the

> . . . solemn troops, and sweet Societies
> That sing, and singing in their glory move. . . .

of *Lycidas,* although in the course of the echoing, "society" has shifted about among the range of meanings listed under *OED* 1 and 2. Phalaris, in any event, is mute and inglorious in a Miltonic way, and the lines anticipate Gray's (published in the following year) in their mode of Miltonic echo as well as in their form, pace, and tone.

This is clearly an echo, and not an allusion. Moreover, it is no mere current tag, itself tied to a gesture of style; the Miltonic presence sounds heavily in the 1740s, and resounds where it has not been asked. An anonymous parodist of William Collins and the Wartons (indeed, perhaps the younger Joseph Warton himself), in attempting to satirize the second, "Il Penseroso"-raddled section of Collins' "Ode on the Poetical Character," produces in 1751 either a deliberate or unwitting, but thoroughly resounding, pastiche of Milton:

> O curfeu-loving Goddess haste,
> O waft me to some *Scythian* waste,
> Where in *Gothic* solitude
> Mid prospects most sublimely rude
> Beneath a rough rock's gloomy chasm
> Thy sister sits *Enthusiasm:*
> Let me with her in magic trance
> Hold most delirious dalliance. . . .[8]

8. These verses quoted from R. S. Crane, ed., *A Collection of English Poems 1660–1800* (New York, 1932), 1238; also see A. S. P. Woodhouse, "Thomas Warton and the 'Ode to Horror,'" *TLS,* January 24, 1929, p. 62, and May 23, 1929, p. 420.

Collins' "Ode to Evening," so famously full of Miltonic echoes and ever attendant upon what the "Poetical Character" ode calls Milton's "evening ear," provides an instructive instance of echoes recollected from more than one point in a region of earlier text. The echo of *Lycidas* ("the Gray-fly winds her sultry horn") in Collins'

> Or where the beetle winds
> Her small but sullen horn

has been widely overheard; the "sullen," however (in its earlier sense of "solemn" and hence, "religious," as well as "moody" and "resonant") comes from "Il Penseroso," where the curfew bell is heard "Over some wide-water'd shore / Swinging slow with sullen roar." The "sullen roar" resounds in the "sullen horn" even as does the "sultry horn." It is the former that, with its complex weight of meaning ("sullen" = melancholy + serious: *or*, "Il Penseroso") explains the force of "small *but* sullen," which is more than merely a question of "small but low-pitched." Whether or not we might want to consider whether Milton's later phrase, in *Lycidas,* is itself an echo of the sound pattern, imprinted in a revision of the trope, of an earlier one (the pastoral-academic version of the unobeyed curfew), Collins seems to have made a montage of the two evening sounds to accompany his own personification of Evening.

Wordsworth, who was so keenly aware of the relation between echo and the voices of the dead, provides an important instance of open acknowledgment of his own practice, in his own note on a poem itself deeply meditative of the eloquence of the past. His "Remembrance of Collins" was not, as the subtitle suggests, "Composed upon the Thames near Richmond," but rather was the result of cutting into two poems a text of five stanzas written years before. The river originally was the Cam, the moment was one of evening boating, the observation directed toward the topos of flowing water as speaking eloquence, and the secondary meditation toward the derivative character of just that theme, itself forming a stream of tradition: "The boat her silent course pursues! / And see how dark the backward stream!" Wordsworth later changed the river to "the Thames near Richmond"—the canonical poetic river of "Prothalamion," and the reflexive, self-referential stream of eloquence of that famous cliché of neoclassicism, the "O could I flow like thee" couplets from Denham's *Cooper's Hill* (see note 4).

Even in the first two stanzas, divided off at Coleridge's suggestion in 1800, the presence of dead poets flickers across a twilit surface. In the stanzas in memory of Collins, who had indeed died some thirty years before, the subtitle is a direct echo of Collins' note to his own poem of 1749, occasioned by the death of James Thomson: "The Scene of the following STANZAS is suppos'd to lie on the *Thames* near *Richmond*." Wordsworth's poem, too, will lie on (as his subtitle will lie about) that particular mythological stretch of water. As we see in the second of these stanzas, it is Collins' relation to Thomson that is shadowed in the water; as we hear in the last lines of the first of them, the view from Cooper's Hill is nearby:

> Glide gently, thus for ever glide,
> O Thames! that other bards may see
> As lovely visions by thy side
> As now, fair river! come to me.
> O glide, fair stream! for ever so,
> Thy quiet soul on all bestowing,
> Till all our minds for ever flow
> As thy deep waters now are flowing.
>
> Vain thought!—Yet be as now thou art,
> That in thy waters may be seen
> The image of a poet's heart,
> How bright, how solemn, how serene!

> Such as did once the Poet bless,
> Who, murmuring here a later ditty,
> Could find no refuge from distress
> But in the milder grief of pity.

In his 1798 note on the "later ditty," Wordsworth points to the echo in the final stanza ("Collins' 'Ode on the death of Thomson,' the last written, I believe, of the poems which were published during his life-time. This Ode is also alluded to in the next stanza.") Collins' second, third, and fourth stanzas move from an avowedly allusive image of the Aeolian harp about which Thomson wrote so famously (here, as a trope for Thomson's poetry itself), to its translation into the natural sound of wind and water music (reeds on a bank). Then, through distancing, we have a ghost of remembrance, discernible only when the mundane water music of the sound of oars is, like that of the abandoned string instrument, suspended:

> II.
> In yon deep Bed of whisp'ring Reeds
>   His airy Harp shall now be laid,
> That He, whose Heart in Sorrow bleeds,
>   May love thro' Life the soothing Shade.

> III.
> Then Maids and Youths shall linger here,
>   And while it's Sounds at distance swell,
> Shall sadly seem in Pity's Ear
>   To hear the WOODLAND PILGRIM'S Knell.

> IV.
> REMEMBRANCE oft shall haunt the Shore
>   When Thames in Summer-wreaths is drest,
> And oft suspend the dashing Oar
>   To bid his gentle Spirit rest!

It is from this region of resonance—sound dying and becoming the trace of memory while the Thames is momentarily undisturbed—that Collins' words rebound. And thus Wordworth's final stanza:

> Now let us, as we float along,
> For *him* suspend the dashing oar;
> And pray that never child of song
> May know that Poet's sorrows more.
> How calm! how still! the only sound,
> The dripping of the oar suspended!
> —The evening darkness gathers round
> By virtue's holiest Powers attended.

But by making the suspended oar drip with an echoing water music, Wordsworth confirms the shadowing of imagery which parallels his echoing. The suspended oar, the emblem of pause and silence in Collins' meditation, becomes the poetic instrument of Wordsworth's allusive one. Indeed, in the eighteenth century, the suspended, abandoned instrument of the metrical versions of Psalm 137 begins to sing again, in refigured fashion, when winds start to blow through it, and it becomes, through long disuse and interpretation, the Aeolian harp. And so with Collins' instrument and Wordsworth's revival of it.

It is instructive to note that Wordworth's "this Ode is also alluded to in the next stanza" glosses the contrastive italicization of "*him*" (Collins, i.e., "himself"). Rhetorically, this is indeed an allusion rather than a proper echo. The understanding of the italicization depends upon an inference, at least, that there is another dashing oar held suspended in the background. But the subtitle is a patent echo, and the scattered fragments of Denham may perhaps be heard in the first stanza. The thematic aspects of the "backward stream" and the "later ditty" make the interrelation of these two poems a clear medium for echo.

With our interpretive figure of the relation of voice and resonant contextual cave in mind, we may observe that even some well-known and often-heard resonances are frequently reechoes, and that allusive fragments occur in chains of rebound. Keats' sonnet "To one who has been long in city pent" is most likely a secondary rebound from the simile of Satan's exultation, in *Paradise Lost* IX, that begins "As one who long in populous city pent" (lines 445ff.) (Emerson's one-line journal entry of 1840, "A man tells a secret for the same reason that he loves the country," glosses most succinctly the connection here between topical and literal, spatial openness.) But the specific link of Satan to the working poet comes from the intermediary echoings of Coleridge, whose revision of Milton Keats probably had read before the Miltonic source itself. In "To the Nightingale" of 1795, Coleridge invokes "Bards in city garret pent" who

> While at their window they with downward eye
> Mark the faint lamp-beam on the kennell'd mud,
> And listen to the drowsy cry of Watchmen
> (Those hoarse unfeather'd Nightingales of Time!),
> How many wretched Bards address *thy* name,
> And hers, the full-orb'd Queen that shines above.

Coleridge's echo of Milton contrasts, incidentally, with his outright quotation from "Il Penseroso" ("'Most musical, most melancholy' Bird!") a few lines further on. It also enlists the prior mythology—of Satan's sense of fresh air as he begins his assault on Paradise—in its own task of reviving the deadened trope of the poetic bird. Two years later on, in "This Lime-Tree Bower My Prison," Coleridge addresses Charles Lamb as having "pined / And hunger'd after Nature, many a year, / In the great City pent. . . ." although here the transfigurative power has been weakened almost into mere allusion.

The final, faint rebound in this chain of echoes is probably Wallace Stevens' in "The Man Whose Pharynx Was Bad,"

where the Miltonic echo voice and the additional returns
from Coleridge and Keats both seem not to cancel each
other but to induce further reverberation. "I am too dumbly
in my being pent," sighs the poet whose syrinx is sad and
silent, who cannot write (and who probably remembers
that Keats could write almost cavalierly of walking in the
resonant country and coming home to read and compose.)[9]

Or let us consider another kind of sequence, one which
leads from an outright scriptural allusion to complex echoes
of a particular interpretation of it in a poem. Ben Jonson, in
the famous Ode to the friendship of Cary and Morison,
praises the latter of the two, who died young, by allusion to
a passage in the Apocrypha (Wisdom of Solomon 11:21):
"Thou hast disposed all nature in measure, number and
weight."

> . . . All offices were done
> By him, so ample, full and round,
> In weight, in measure, number, sound

But in the next strophe of the ode, we are reminded that life
is measured for its quality, not its mere duration; the trope in
these later lines is of art for life, the well-wrought quality of
the poem of a man's days, and it concludes at the precise
center of the "Ode":

> For life doth her great actions spell,
> By what was done and wrought
> In season, and so brought
> To light: her measures are, how well
> Each syllabe answered, and was framed, how fair;
> These make the lines of life, and that's her air.

The text from Wisdom is widely cited in the Renaissance—
indeed, its importance goes back to St. Augustine. But this

9. Harold Bloom has suggested to me the additional erotic resonance of
Whitman's line "From pent-up, aching rivers. . . ." here, in a context of
loss of voice.

way of interpreting it, through the prosodic senses of the words (quantity, syllable, accentuation, reinforced by the association of lines of verse and life-lines in palmistry) is peculiarly Jonsonian. (As opposed, for example, to the reading of Henry Reynolds, quoting Pico della Mirandola in *Mythomystes*: " . . . God . . . did nothing by chance, but through his wisdome disposed all things as in weight measure, so likewise in number"—the point being to justify cabbalistic numerology.) Abraham Cowley adduces the same text in a note to his line from the biblical epic *Davideis* (I, 451), "Such was God's poem, this World's new Essay"; he comments, "And the *Scripture* witnesses, that the World was made in *Number, Weight* and *Measure*; which are all Qualities of a good *Poem*."

When Andrew Marvell alludes to the same scriptural passage at the end of his remarkable prefatory poem to the second edition of *Paradise Lost,* Jonson's application of it and Cowley's further treatment, not to speak of his ordering of the terms, both read and sound through the lines. Agreeing that Milton need not apologize for using blank verse, Marvell asserts, "Thy verse created like thy theme sublime / In number, weight and measure needs not rhyme." Marvell's poem becomes, at its close, a Jonsonian fit of rhyme against rhyme (replete with a joke turning on use and mention). It includes a subtle but brilliant echo of Miltonic linear style, in voicing an earlier fear, as he began to read it, that *Paradise Lost* might seem a failure, wondering "Through that wide field how he his way should find / O'er which lame faith leads understanding blind." The first of these lines recalls the celebrated monosyllabic lines of *Paradise Lost* ("Rocks, caves, lakes, fens, bogs, dens, and shades of death," for example), the second, Milton's characteristic figurative use of what is traditionally only the scheme of chiasmus (as in the lines following the one just quoted—"A universe of death, which God by curse / Created evil, for evil only good, / Where all life dies, death lives. . . ." or in "The hell within him, for within him Hell / He brings"). Even the enjambment of Marvell's final lines is echoic of a verse of *Paradise Lost,* "sublime" being syntactically ambiguous as to whether it is absolute or "sublime in number, etc.," and the ambiguity is dramatically and heuristically controlled by the line break. In any event, Marvell takes the reader, as Milton takes Satan in his monosyllabic lines, through the same journey of reading (this poem is in part Marvell's "On First Looking into Milton's Bible") on which he has himself set out. In this context of the figurative treatment of poetic form, of meter for moral matter, the force of *create* to apply to *verse* in the penultimate line is intensified, and the echoic quality of the allusion—resounding from the cave of Jonson's trope of prosody and virtue—confirmed.

It is this trope of the scriptural passage interpreted morally through the median image of poetic form to which Blake is so sensitive, in his ironic echo of Marvell in one of the Proverbs of Hell: "Bring out number, weight and measure [these might almost have inverted commas about them—they are so clearly in Marvell's word order] in a year of dearth." In a condition of plenitude, implies Blake's Devil, there is no need to mete and dole. Had man and nature not fallen, there would be no need for poems like *Paradise Lost* to teach us why and how they did, poems whose freedom from the bondage of rhyming could only lead to a higher and more sublime prosodic and visionary bondage. In proceeding from Jonson to Blake the echo rebounds from the figurative special use of "number, weight and measure" as terms from *ars poetica*.

Another sequence of reechoing is struck up by Spenser's name for Acrasia's pretty but bad garden in *The Faerie Queene,* Book II. The Bower of Bliss "Of her fond favorites so nam'd amis" becomes a true earthly paradise, a legitimate if momentary fallen replacement of a lost unity of nature and man, when the words of its name are reversed in order. In "Prothalamion," Spenser invokes

> Ye gentle birdes, the worlds faire ornament,
> And heavens glorie, whom this happie hower
> Doth leade unto your lovers blissful bower.

It is this Spenserian inversion—of the name of the false inversion of the place of love—which Milton echoes in *Paradise Lost,* Book IV. Adam and Eve prepare to go to bed, having just been discussing the audible echoes of the music of the spheres in paradise:

> Thus talking hand in hand alone they pass'd
> On to the blissful bower; it was a place
> Chos'd by the sovran Planter, when he framed
> All things to man's delightful use.

Just how resonant this phrase is—glancing off the almost heavenly bird song in Spenser's context, resounding against the inversion already present in Spenser's own self-echoing—can best be heard when we contrast it with an outright ironic allusion to the original, unreconstructed Bower of Bliss. Thomas Carew's great erotic poem, *A Rapture,* is echoic primarily of Donne in the *Elegies.* But at one point a brilliant pair of allusions, one biblical, one Spenserian, is introduced as if hyperbolically, yet with a deeper, figurative purpose. The poet, inviting his far from heavenly Celia to fly with him to "Love's Elysium," likens himself at the start of one long passage to "the empty bee, that lately bore / Into the common measure all her store," flying about the field from flower to flower, but moving in metaphor from place to place on a body that is to be the earth of Celia's. He will

> taste the ripened cherry,
> The warm, firm apple, tipped with coral berry;

> Then will I visit with a wandering kiss
> The vale of lilies, and the bower of bliss.

The echoic reversal of the "lily of the valley" from the Song of Songs substitutes place on a person for the biblical trope of person in a place. (Indeed, this flickering back and forth between body in garden and garden in body is one of the complex strategies of Carew's whole masterpiece.) The name of Acrasia's bower tells its own lie against the negative moral force of the original place-name, unveiling its almost sarcastic quality in Spenser. It goes a step further, too, in naming a topos on a figurative body—the valley between the breasts—with the name of a poetic topos, the whole body itself being present only in the figure of the field of flowers "that dwell / In my delicious paradise." Spenser's own later use of the phrase in *Amoretti* 76 to describe the lady's bosom ("The bowre of blisse, the paradice of plea-sure") is surely allusive and ironic, as a figure of the garden for the poet's sweet, winged thoughts. Particularly as that figure is developed in the following sonnet, the allusiveness has both a private and a public revisionary force. But it is a gentle revision, whereas Carew's echo is an outright denial of the meaning of the original voice, whose scene or cave of resonance is the artificiality and deadliness of the delights of Acrasia's place. His poem is a magnificent struggle to main-tain Satan's inadvertent fiction mentioned earlier, that Adam and Eve are "imparadist in one another's arms." (They are, in fact, still in literal Paradise, with no need for the prostheses of passion or of trope.) It seems only subcon-sciously aware—in the sense that poems seem to have awareness—of the power of Spenser's taxonomy of true and false fictional paradises, aware that erotic exuberance is somehow as desperate as, say, a royalist cause.

The trope of echo—if so it be—seems so essentially Miltonic a device that it is not surprising to find Milton himself unusually sensitive to its operation. The very youthful poet, with no style of his own yet and no characteristic voice, cannot truly be said to echo in our sense. In the very bad opening line of his first English poem (the one on the death of the Fair Infant), there is no particular Elizabethan voice, and no echoing cell, in "O fairest flower, no sooner blown but blasted." (It is a line almost worthy of Peter Quince's play, a little magazine of clichés.) But in the next two lines, the young Milton moves ontogenetically forward: "Summer's chief honour if thou hadst outlasted / Bleak winter's force that made thy blossom drie." There is no allusion here. But what we hear is gathered from the *stanze* of Shakespeare's sonnets, *passim.* Twelve years later, when rewriting his earlier draft of *Lycidas,* Milton was sufficiently conscious of echoing to revise at least one line in order to cancel a trace of voice that he possibly only heard on rereading. "Bring the rath primrose that unwedded dies" must have resounded too loudly with a line from that speech in *The Winter's Tale* which reverberates throughout the whole passage of floral-poetical "false surmise" in *Lycidas:* "Pale primroses / That die unmarried ere they can behold / Bright Phoebus in their strength." To damp this overhang, Milton made the primrose "forsaken" rather than "unwedded," and the loudest echo vanished. But we may still take note of the scene of generation of the wider, barely audible echo here—the discussion of nature and art between Perdita and Polixenes, and her floral tribute to Florizel, not "like a corse," but "like a bank for love to lie and play on"; or, if so, "not to be buried, but quick and in mine arms." Even to make a further figurative use of such a conceit is, for Milton, "false surmise." Flowers will have to be more radically transformed, and poesy more powerfully quickened, than that.

Here is another series of relayed echoes in the course of which the transmission occurs, as almost always, through an interpretation. Satan, we are told in *Paradise Lost* I (211–15), would have remained "chain'd on the burning Lake" forever, had not God "left him at large to his own dark designs." William Cowper, struggling against madness and the anxious solitude of doubt, composed one of his most powerful hymns to a dark Providence which nobody but a fatuous, Job-comforting, simpleton of the spirit could proclaim to be patently manifest:

> God moves in a mysterious way
>   His wonders to perform;
> He plants his footsteps in the sea,
>   And rides upon the storm.
>
> Deep in unfathomable mines
>   Of never-failing skill,
> He treasures up his bright designs,
>   And works his sovereign will. . . .

In Cowper's *Olney Hymns* XXXV ("Light Shining Out of Darkness"), the willed struggle with the dialectic of Providence in Milton ("As He our darkness, cannot we his Light / Imitate when we please?" asks Mammon the gold miner in Book II, as he begins to argue for his touching parody of the Protestant ethic) works through his antithetical echo, operating the implicit contrastive device of so much wisdom literature (see chapter 2). This may or may not be a source of the speaker's voice in Blake's "The Tyger," with its concern for immortal and dread hands, eyes, and feet. But given some of the subsequent stanzas, it is hard to avoid the evocation of a secondary concern, a parable about reading parables of Providence:

> Judge not the Lord by Feeble sense,
>   But trust him for his grace:
> Behind a frowning providence
>   He hides a smiling face. . .

> Blind unbelief is sure to err,
>   And scan his work in vain:
> God is his own interpreter,
>   And he will make it plain.

Certainly if we go back to the Miltonic passage, we can hear rebounds of a wider timbre: the "dark designs" would lead Satan, "with reiterated crimes" to "heap on himself damnation, while he sought / Evil to others, and enrag'd might see / How all his malice serv'd but to bring forth / Infinite goodness . . ." (I, 214–18). Satan's dark designs are the underground form of God's bright ones, which will only gleam when they come to light, or in this case, to white.

Richard Poirier has shown most persuasively the influence of William James' *Pragmatism* on the use of the word *design* in Robert Frost's "In White," the 1912 draft of what would be rewritten as the famous "Design" with its antepenultimate question "What but design of darkness to appall?" The early version reads "What but design of darkness and of night?" but in both instances, the antithetical echo of Cowper's almost proverbial lines takes one back again to Cowper's relation to Milton. A cycle of readings of the manifest and the latent in brightness and darkness has been completed, as a cycle of unreeling Protestant faith is played out: even the death of God leaves the problem of Providence as mysterious as it ever was. Frost was probably responding to the lines about God's interpretation of the texts of the world and Himself as much as to the rest of the hymn in his echo. In the last line of "In White," however ("Design, design! Do I use the word aright?"), he is *alluding* to the pages of James he had been reading.

The fragmentations and breakings-off of intertextual echo can result in pieces of voice as small as single words, and as elusive as particular cadences. The reappearance of particular words has long been acknowledged by the apparatus of scholia, although the tendency of annotators, employing the genially open philological "Cf.," has been to shun the caves of ambiance and the chambers of meaning. Shelley's boyhood companionship with the west wind, "When to outstrip thy skiey speed / Scarce seemed a vision" has to recall, ultimately, the disguised Duke's counsel to Claudio in *Measure for Measure* (III, i) when life is to be addressed as "a breath . . . / Servile to all the skyey influences." Indeed, most early echoes of the Shakespeare passage (with its unique early occurrence of the word) seem to be outright quotations or acknowledged allusions. But poetically echoing words get passed about in what are frequently less immediate ways. I would suggest that Shelley may have been remembering an early poem of Coleridge's, the "Lines on an Autumnal Evening" of 1793, in which storms, "the troubles of the air," are "the skiey deluge, and white lightning's glare." The context of autumnal wind may be modulating the echo here. (Shelley may have been remembering this same poem in translating a line from Plato's epigram on Astêr—"Ouranos hôs pollois ommasin eis se blepô"—as "To look upon thee with a thousand eyes.") But the terraced echoes of Shakespeare's phrase can be traced in the *OED* entry on "skyey," and readers may consider the range of true resonance in the quotations and allusions.

Unpremeditated is another Miltonic word—about his muse, who "dictates to me slumb'ring, or inspires / Easy my unpremeditated Verse" (*Paradise Lost* IX, 23–24)— whose Shelleyan echo is instructive. The skylark pours out its full heart "In profuse strains of unpremeditated art," and the trace of the voice of Miltonic invocation awakens an additional resonance of the theme, in the invocation of Book III, of metaphorical poetic light come out of darkness in the music of the nightingale and of blind bards and prophets. The mythopoeia of Shelley's "To a Sky-Lark" is to make of the bird whose powerfully shrilling song seems to come from the whole sky above—rather than from some tiny speck, too insignificant to produce such sound—a day-time analogue of the nightingale. The Miltonic "unpremeditated" art that comes out of the night is being refigured in Shelley's mode of unpremeditation, and sounds with a later meaning in Shelley's echo.

And so, too, with the complementary word from the complementary Miltonic invocation to Book III:

> Then feed on thoughts, that voluntary move
> Harmonious numbers; as the wakeful Bird
> Sings darkling, and in shadiest Covert hid
> Tunes her nocturnal Note . . . .   (37–40)

And so Keats, at a crucial moment of turn in the structure of the images of the "Ode to a Nightingale": "Darkling, I listen. . . ." The word is transformed in the echo, not merely by being applied to the response rather than to the act of eloquence, but by including in its sound somehow an acknowledgment of the source, as if to say "Darkling, I listen as Milton's wakeful Bird / Sings darkling" and even, "Darkling, I listen to Milton's *darkling*." It is the cave of creativity-as-response from which the nymph calls here, as well as the neighboring one of song-out-of-darkness. In Matthew Arnold, there is a systematic emptying of the word of its echoes. He seizes upon it, in "Dover Beach," in a mode of relatively hollow allusion; and will not grant what Keats heard in it, and has us overhear.

On the other hand, there is Thomas Hardy's "The Darkling Thrush," that powerful modernist replacement for a secular masque, a wake over "the century's corpse," which was originally entitled "By the Century's Death-bed" in 1900. It adds the echoing title as an afterthought, but as a profound gloss as well. Neither season nor landscape, in the first stanzas of Hardy's poem, offer any visions of a heroic or promising future: that the New Year comes just past midwinter is design of darkness enough, and nature presents only unavailable romantic emblems of worldly harmony and beauty: "The tangled bine-stems scored the sky / Like strings of broken lyres." It is amid this unpromising erasure of possibilities for the sublime that the "agèd thrush, frail gaunt and small" presents himself, and as the revised title acknowledges, he appears as a poetic avatar of the darkling nightingales and poets, and even the skylark (he "had chosen thus to fling his soul / Upon the growing gloom). Just as the image of the bird is a complex, consciously late reworking of the Miltonic and romantic images, so does the word *darkling* seem to bring new meanings in revision of the older ones. We are back to Milton insofar as the bird, rather than the hearer, is darkling, and back to Milton if we take this poem, as I do, as embodying the record of an intimate vocation, a call for Hardy to emerge more publicly as a poet. But the Arnoldian usage—of *darkening* —applies to the world, not the condition of the poet or the bird. One reads the dark, the other sings out of it, and the song has at least echoes in it of a song of hope, echoes that allow the interpreting poet some figurative wherewithal to fancy their presence.

One might note in passing that the Shelleyan phrase "Be thou me, impetuous one" from the "West Wind" ode echoes in Wallace Stevens in just such a strange way, almost as if there had been an intervening rebound. In the bird song canto (vi) of "It Must Change" in *Notes Toward a Supreme Fiction,*

> Bethou me, said sparrow to the crackled blade,
> And you, and you, bethou me as you blow,
> When in my coppice you behold me be.

Here, as has frequently been observed, the phrase, still an imperative, becomes a nonce term for *tutoyer.* And yet it is accompanied, as if with the closely following single resound of an electronic echo chamber, by the original meaning.

Indeed, as is so often the case with Stevens' ambiguous constructions, it is the relation between the two or more possible meanings that itself not only enters their array, but seems to dominate them. What is the state of affairs existing between a poet and his trope when the trope talks like the poet in the first place and, in the second, when that figurative bird could become one with what it addresses (by getting that windy object to address it in the grammatical form of a kind of imaginative familiar second person)? The hovering of the echo here is perhaps enhanced by the secondary echo of Hardy, in the "coppice" (Hardy's "coppice-gate" rather than, say, the more normal "copse").

Unlike old refrains, whose signification may die away through constant reuse in *contrafactum* (unless reinterpreted through satiric reworking or openly allusive evocativeness), echoes of single words grow in volume. Sometimes, after a series of rebounds of the kinds mentioned above, the final sound will have the quality of summing up the whole series of resonances. Consider, for example, the penultimate line of Hart Crane's "At Melville's Tomb": "Monody shall not wake the mariner." Melville's own title, "Monody," (for his elegy on the dead Hawthorne) itself echoes the subtitle of *Lycidas* ("In this Monody, the Author . . ."), even though there is no hint of drowning in Melville's imagery. Crane's poem is a different matter. The sea in his elegy is, with a characteristic ellipsis of "far and———," described as "wide from this ledge," and the distance between tomb and sea is that between fact and fable. Melville becomes the drowned sailor in Crane's poem, and the "monody" is, by allusion, Melville's for Hawthorne, and, in echo, the mode of *Lycidas*. Indeed, the "mariner" of the same line may be an echo of the title phrase of Raymond Weaver's *Herman Melville: Mariner and Mystic* (1921), that groundbreaking study which had appeared four or five years before.

Philosophy—for which the writer's voice is always more a utensil, at best, than a material—is full of derived, quoted, and otherwise allusive uses of single words; and yet when one philosophical writer uses a precursor's word, it is a concept or a meaning, or a use that he is employing. When poetic echoes are only of one word—one word echoed completely, as a mountain echo might return a monosyllabic word in its entirety—one might be tempted to suggest that here too only one *sense* of the word was being allusively invoked. Consider, for example, Wordsworth's Laodamia, addressing the Phantom of her dead husband, Protesilaus: "Redundant are thy locks, thy lips as fair / As when their breath enriched Thessalian air" ("Laodamia," lines 59–60). The Miltonic word is the one used in the description of Satan "enclos'd / In Serpent" (IX, 494–503), "not with indented wave, / Prone on the ground, as since" but in a parody of rectitude, a vertical coil embodying the amazements of error, "erect / Amidst his circling Spires, that on the grass / Floated redundant: pleasing was his shape, / And lovely. . . ." It is by ironic contrast with the fallen "crooked" pattern of "indented wave" that Milton underlines the unfallen stem *unda* in *redundant,* and Wordsworth's use of it to mean "wavy" might be considered, as suggested above, merely a Miltonic sort of etymological use.

But I think not. There seem to be other echoes of the demonic regions of *Paradise Lost* in Wordsworth's classical fable. Phrases like "such love as Spirits feel / In worlds whose course is equable and pure" ("Laodamia," 97–98), which conjures up Raphael's seminar, or "Spake of heroic arts in graver mood / Revived, with finer harmony pursued" (101–2), which resounds with Book II of *Paradise Lost,* combine turns of syntax in association with words and manifest subject. So does the way in which the Greek heroes "Prepared themselves for glorious enterprise / By martial sports, —or, seated in the tent, / Chieftains and kings in

council were detained" (117–19). It is as if, in order to con-
jure up a classical scene and avoid the slippery slope into
neoclassicism, Wordsworth were clinging to the demonic
prefiguration of classical antiquity in the culture of Pandemonium. Pope's use, in his *Odyssey,* of the etymologized
Miltonic word—"Floats in bright waves redundant o'er the
ground" (XVIII, 342) has none of the echoing quality of
Wordsworth's. In "Laodamia" the whole range of images of
waviness in *Paradise Lost* has been evoked: the brooks in
Paradise, "With mazy error under pendant shades" (IV,
239), Adam and Eve's hair (IV, 301–11), the curling of vines
adduced both of the latter and in Book V, 215ff, the comical
curl of elephantine trunk (IV, 345–47)—all of these unfallen
emblems come from the waviness of hair itself, rather than
that of water, for whose sensuousness Milton does not appear to have felt much. Wordsworth has gathered up these
meanings in his phantom of the temporarily reconstituted
dead hero, and the shades of moralizing of the fable are
delicately summoned up by the tone of Miltonic voice.

Very often, a single word is echoed in conjunction with a
rhymed or assonant one, so that we have the effect of a
whole phrase being transmitted, partly in clear focus and
partly blurred. Again, from the Keats "Nightingale" ode,
"the viewless wings" of poetry may, as has been noted, echo
Milton's bad poem, "The Passion" ("thence hurried on
viewless wing"). Angus Fletcher has observed that "viewless" in *Comus* seems to come from Claudio's speech about
death in *Measure for Measure* III, i: "To be imprison'd in the
viewless winds, / And blown with restless violence round
about / The pendent world"; but in "The Passion" (and,
either thereby or directly) to Keats, the movement is from
"viewless winds" to "viewless wings." There can be no
doubt about the power of the Shakespearean passage for
Milton's ear, at any rate: the "pendent world" itself reap-

pears directly in *Paradise Lost,* at the end of Book II (line 1052), awaiting Satan's violence and his gift of death.

A single word or phrase, then, amplified or not by a phonetic scheme, may easily carry rumors of its resounding cave. So, too, can those schemes and patterns themselves if given originally a charge of significance. When Samson, in his great opening speech in *Samson Agonistes,* echoes *Paradise Lost,* the consequences of his rhetoric are as profound as they are within the earlier epic itself—as when Satan echoes the narration or Adam, Satan. The blind hero, ruminating his ruin, aware that when a fortress crumbles it can become a dark prison, asks what strength is "without a double share / Of wisdom." He answers himself: "Vast, unwieldly, burdensome, / Proudly secure, yet liable to fall / By weakest subtleties." God's "Sufficient to have stood, yet free to fall" (of the newly-created Adam, III, 99), is itself echoed unwittingly by Adam in his injunction to Eve in Book IX (line 360): "Firm we subsist, yet possible to swerve." This whole speech, in which Samson is continually misreading his predicament, is tinged with an earlier tone of casuistry: Satan's sleazy rhetoric in Book X in boasting to his hissing companions employs the mendacious specificity of a carnival barker or snake-oil salesman: "Him by fraud I have seduc'd / From his Creator, and the more to increase / Your wonder, with an Apple" (lines 485–87). Just so Samson's misplaced concreteness in his own self-deluding dialectic: "God, when he gave me strength, to show withal / How slight the gift was, hung it in my Hair." (*Samson Agonistes,* 58–59).

Often such echoes of figure or phrase pattern can be maddeningly elusive. I. A. Richards' overhearing of Tennyson's "Tithonus" sighing behind the first refrain line of William Empson's villanelle, "Missing Dates" (mentioned earlier, in footnote 2 to this chapter) raises interesting questions about Echo's acoustical abilities, as it were:

EMPSON: The waste remains, the waste remains and kills
TENNYSON: *The woods decay, the woods decay and fall*

This rebound gives back neither word nor phrase, but instead a kind of cadence, involving phonemic and semantic elements, locked in a syntactic and metrical pattern. The musical ear can be said—as it was by Leibniz—to perform a kind of unconscious arithmetic in its recognitions of timbres, and the infant speaker to exhibit complex wonders of linguistic competence. So, too, the overhearing ear in this instance is, in effect, recognizing the following awkwardly represented schema:

The w⸺ —e̊—åy, the w⸺ —e̊—åy, and ⸺ll (i.e. dies)

The echo uses the pattern more strongly, as if somehow thereby to increase its volume: the vowel of *waste* is that of the repeated third word; the shift of the verbs to transitivity and the subsequent number correction of "kills" strengthen the new line, and exercise that strange power of usurping originality that we have seen in influential echoes throughout these remarks. The relation between voice and echo here is one of slow, splendid vision to hardheaded assessment of consequences. The lines might be connected as "(Tennyson), and, yes, (Empson)." Certainly this is a true echo. But it is like hearing a rhythm in return.[10]

Far more elusive is the ghost of a slightly earlier cadence which plays through a line from Allen Tate's "Ode to the

10. Empson himself reaffirms this melody in another villanelle line, "It is the pain, it is the pain endures." But Tennyson's line is itself full of echo. Christopher Ricks points out in his edition of Tennyson (London, 1969, p. 1114) that it originally read, "Ay me, ay me! the woods decay and fall," and that the revision was influenced by Wordsworth: "the immeasurable height / Of woods decaying, never to be decayed" (*The Prelude* VI, 624–25). The way in which echoing texts rebound is somewhat like electromagnetic induction of a current; this is only one instance in which the echo pattern, or scheme, evokes the allusive trope.

Confederate Dead," a poem full of the beauty of broken echoes:

> Autumn is desolation in the plot
> [Beauty is momentary in the mind ——Stevens,
> "Peter Quince at the Clavier"]
> Of a thousand acres where these memories grow
> From the inexhaustible bodies that are not
> Dead, but feed the grass, row after rich row.

The Stevensian cadence resounds in our reading, even though other echoes inhabit the garden of these words. The modernist formula, popularized by W. C. Williams in his poems of the early twenties, of identifying programmatically an abstraction (emotion, state) with an emblem of it—almost with the iconographic certainty of a modernist Ripa—produced characteristic phrases like "Sorrow is my own yard" ("The Widow's Lament in Springtime"), "Old age is / a flight of small / cheeping birds" ("To Waken an Old Lady"), or the title of "The Attic Which Is Desire." Tate's yoking of the two abstractions in this wise, as if the "desolation" were more concrete, is plangent and beautiful. So is his use of enjambment to quicken the meaning of "not / Dead."

Tate's four lines conclude with an echo of the violent use of negation as a predicate that we get in a couplet from Donne's "Nocturnall upon St. Lucie's Day": "He ruin'd me; and I am re-begot / Of absence, darknesse, death, things which are not." The stressed rhymed and metrical position of Donne's monosyllable makes us take it as a nonce adjective (for "partaking of not-ness"), rather than a negative particle ("aren't"). Tate echoes and then smothers the echo in his enjambment, claiming the move for his own voice. Here again, the Miltonic device allows two readings to hover across the contre-rejet. Apart from the constant sound of Eliot in the poem, there is the significant whisper of Hart Crane in the latter's almost mannered form of construction (Tate's ". . . the splayed leaves / Pile up, of nature the casual sacrament" suggests Crane's *moderne* inversions like "and of Gargantua, the laughter" in "Praise for an Urn"). It is strange to hear also, in this line and a half, a kind of echo revised—again from "Peter Quince at the Clavier," the concluding "And makes a constant sacrament of praise." But there is another point of resonance to account for this, the constant topical matter of eternizing in poetry aside. The syntax of Stevens' line, in its "of + noun" phrase, is ambiguous in a way typical of the language of *Harmonium*. It can read either "And makes a constant sacrament that is praise" or "And makes, out of praise, a constant sacrament," so that perhaps Tate's line uses the inversion to exact one of these readings from the low throbbing of ambiguity. In any event, the regions of resonance of all these possible anterior voices—the Donne "Nocturnall," "Peter Quince," and Crane's "Praise for an Urn"—are well within the boundaries of the topos of Tate's "Ode." So are the Shelleyan-Miltonic leaves (see the discussion of Milton's simile of dead leaves in Chapter 4), just as Crane's "well-meant idioms" at the end of "Praise for an Urn" are, echoing Shelley, to be "scattered." (Tate's mention of Shelley in his famous discussion of the poem, "Narcissus as Narcissus," all but avows the echo.)

Let us examine a few more instances of scattered echoing. We have already observed how Keats gathered material from several lines of Milton's "Nativity" ode for his poem to Psyche. Wallace Stevens always shows a great command of the dynamic range of echo, from the almost blatantly allusive to the most muted and problematic of phantoms. In "Across the unscrawled fores the future casts / And throws his stars around the floor. . . ." from *Notes Toward a Supreme Fiction* ("It Must Be Abstract" III, 16–17), the echo of Shelley, from *The Defence of Poetry*—"the gigantic shadows that futurity casts over the present"—lurks. It is even susceptible of being amplified by the hearing aid of external evidence (i.e., the passage in question in the checked and underlined copy of Shelley's essay in Stevens' copy of an Everyman volume, edited by Ernest Rhys, called "Defences of Poetry"). On the other hand, far more ghostly is the shade of Valéry, elsewhere in the opening canto of *Notes,* in ". . . nor for that mind compose / A voluminous master folded in his fire," ("It Must Be Abstract" I, 8–9), where "Midi le juste y compose de feu / La mer, la mer toujours recommencée" (of "Le Cimitière marin") appears to hover, because of the exposed and emphasized terminal, pseudorhyming, positions of *compose* and *fire.* Such is a true ghost: like all phenomena of this sort, we must always wonder what our own contribution was—how much we are always being writers as well as readers of what we are seeing.

Merely ghost*ly,* but certainly manifesting the authentic presence of an earlier voice, is the self-echoed phrase from "Sunday Morning": "As a calm darkens among waterlights / Moving across wide water, without sound. / The day is like wide water without sound. . . ." Given the transmitted echo, the force of the reflexive one is such that we should perhaps analyze the second of these lines as "The day is like 'wide water without sound.'" That transmitted echo is from one of the most resonant passages in "Il Penseroso":

> Oft on a plat of rising ground,
> I hear the far-off *Curfew* sound,
> Over some wide-water'd shore,
> Swinging slow with sullen roar.   (lines 73–76)

I have already discussed this echo, along with the Tennysonian "half-awakened birds," in another place,[11] but I want

11. See my *Vision and Resonance* (New York and London, 1976), 158–60; also 131–33.

to reconsider it now with respect to the region of signification from which the original voice rebounds. The relation of Milton's *penseroso* poet to the neglected but considered curfew is that of the imaginative consciousness to a sign that is presented univocally (i.e., the curfew "means" *stop walking about and go home now*). But the nightwalker, himself sensible of the strange interpenetration of sight and sound at the moment of darkening, misreads the sign equivocally (or, as an earlier critical generation might have put it, "esthetically"). So, too, is Stevens' protagonist, ignoring some church bell, perhaps (unheard in the poem) considering ("she dreams a little") the consequences of "that old catastrophe" among whose catastrophic consequences remains the literal fact of death. The figures are analogous, and the echo profoundly resonant.

We have seen that fragments need not be ghostly. George Meredith provides Stevens with a significant phrase in "Le Monocle de Mon Oncle" through the title of his "Ballad of Past Meridian" (Stevens: "No spring can follow past meridian"). Meredith himself almost alludes to, I should say, rather than echoes, Emerson's phrase "the Lords of Life" (from the verse epigraph to "Experience") as he firmly clutches the words in order to deny the trope they name with an implicit contrast. "We are the lords of life, and life is warm" uneasily, and wrongly, asserts the speaker in one of the bitterest sonnets (XXX) of *Modern Love,* a poem Stevens seems to keep hearing from time to time in his later redaction of some of it, "Le Monocle." The following passage might be exhibited (under the heading of the *Unheimliche Vorklänge?*) as an example of ghostly anticipation:

> A quiet company we pace, and wait
> The dinner-bell in prae-digestive calm.
> So sweet up violet banks the Southern balm
> Breathes round, we care not if the bell be late:

> Though here and there grey seniors question Time
> In irritable coughings . . .

> <div align="right">(<i>Modern Love,</i> XXXVII)</div>

A word might be said about the general case of the anticipatory, or apparently reversed, echo of Stevens in such lines as these—which, save for an inversion and the spelling of *prae-digestive* might come from a canceled draft of "Le Monocle de Mon Oncle."

I have in another context discussed lines by John Clare and D. G. Rossetti that "anticipate" the cadences of Robert Frost.[12] Consider such apparent hauntings as the sound of Emily Dickinson in

> It cannot vault, or dance, or play,
> It never was in *France* or *Spain;*
> Nor can it entertain the day
> With my great stable or demain:

> (Herbert, "The Quidditie")

or of Frost's "Never Again Would Birds' Song Be the Same" in George Meredith's lines on another poet: "but in his lyric had a tone / As 'twere the forest-echo of her voice." In these and similar instances, phantasms of what Harold Bloom has called, in *The Anxiety of Influence,* the stance of *apophrades,* or "return of the dead," there is no need for hermeneutic fear. They are, I think, merely instances of echo so scattered in the later texts that they seem to be regathered, in a reversal of direction, in the earlier one (aside from the possibility, that is, of a more direct echo, say, of the Herbert lines in Dickinson's "I never saw a moor"). And again, this may be a point at which echoing blends into the more general drone of stylistic transmission.[13]

---

12. *Vision and Resonance,* p. 105.

13. This way of combining scattered echoed voices might be worth studying as a particular allusive mode. Milton's famous "No light, but rather Darkness visible" (*Paradise Lost* I, 63) is simply echoed in Whittier's

This bidirectional quality of echo is frequently at work in major poetry, where in the structure of the poem's rhetoric, the anterior voice is made to seem the echo of the present one. This is itself a trope of *hysteron proteron* (rather than merely the usual grammatical scheme of it), or of the *pre-posterous* (literally). When used dramatically, relations between texts aside, it can have poignancy as well as power. Andrew Marvell's Damon the Mower, as he "among the grass fell down, / By his own scythe, the mower mown," reflects that although his wound will heal, his pain of erotic longing will not: "'Tis death alone that this must do: / For Death thou art a Mower too." Death, like all readers of these lines, would want to put it the other way around. So does the whole tradition of imagery that the poem engages: Death is The Mower, and Damon is a mower too. It is like the antiplatonic reversal in which the individual proclaims its material reality against the paradigmatic ghostliness of mere ideas. Marvell is here playing delicately with the touching and callow egocentrism of lovers' metaphysical games, and it is most interesting that *mower* means "mocker" (*OED* Mower[2]), and that "the mower mown" is also thereby "the mocker mocked." Given my general subject, by the way, I would add that the strength of the topoi—flesh as grass, time and death as mowers—tends perhaps to drown out the likelihood of an echo of Marvell's voice in the line characterizing the mower's "whistling scythe" rebounding in Robert Frost's early "Mowing": "My long scythe whispered, and left the hay to make." It is

---

Snowbound in the "unwarming light, / Which only seemed where'er it fell / To make the coldness visible." But in the final version of D. H. Lawrence's great "Bavarian Gentians," the "Persephone herself is but a voice / Or a darkness invisible enfolded in the deeper dark" blends this echo with that of "O dark, dark, dark / Amid the blaze of noon" from *Samson Agonistes* (this echoes throughout the poem).

at any rate clear that the scythe in the later poem whispers not "death!" in the voice of Whitman's birds, but the text from Isaiah about flesh being like grass, which lies behind both his poem and Marvell's.

Another ghostly demarcation: Meredith, in "A Later Alexandrian," is ostensibly characterizing Rossetti's poetry; but in the following lines, it is a momentary tone of pure Tennyson (from "Mariana") that we hear, not the Tennyson in Rossetti:

> The moon of cloud discoloured was his Muse,
> His pipe the reed of the old moaning waste
> (Tennyson: "Upon the lonely moated grange")

The fussy inversion of the first line is in Meredith's own, and Rossetti's occasional, tone. But the wail of the second one is not.

Familiar resounding in Eliot's *The Waste Land* indeed raises another interesting problem: that of the relative degree to which allusions and echoes are acknowledged—implicitly or explicitly—by authors, and whether in the text or in scholia or commentary. The vast allusive apparatus of *The Waste Land* might be renamed "these echoes I have shored against ruin," for its heap of broken images contains both smashed *eidola* (Baconian and Whitmanian) and entire figures broken off, or away from, their bases and backgrounds. The mode of acknowledgment in the notes added on later is most evasive, in itself. Not only is accreditation peculiarly supplied (for example, the epigraph from Petronius, added after the canceled original epigraph from *Heart of Darkness,* had already been noticed, selected, and isolated in both prose and verse translation by D. G. Rossetti long before). It is almost as if a kind of suppression were at work in the texture of recognition and avowal, a nod to allusion but not to echo.

Thus, the Tennysonian "a handful of dust" (line 30) is undoubtedly from *Maud:* "Dead, dead, long dead / And my heart is a handful of dust / And the wheels go over my head." The conscious echoes of Tennyson's "Ulysses" were expunged in the deletion (at Pound's suggestion) of most of the original lines of the "Death by Water" section. A strong resounding suggestion of poetic drowning still remains, however, in an otherwise totally puzzling detail. Earlier, in Part II, we have been made to see a travesty of the "sylvan scene" of *Paradise Lost* IV, 140, in the Thracian woods, locus of "the change of Philomel, by the barbarous king / So rudely forced" (lines 98–100). Now, at line 204, we hear a strange echo, unexplained in the notes, of a prior voice, occurring at a point of acknowledged repetition (in the note to line 100) of an earlier phrase:

> Twit twit twit
> Jug jug jug jug jug jug
> So rudely forc'd.   (lines 203–5)

The voice of the ravished nightingale returns here, but the bird is no longer Ovidian: she smacks now of the wakeful bird who "sings darkling, and in shadiest Covert hid / Tunes her nocturnal note." There is nothing to explain the peculiar spelling "forc'd" at this point except a Miltonic echo, in covert hid: "And with forc'd fingers rude" (*Lycidas,* line 4). The milieu of the drowned poet is a sufficiently resonant cave here, and the note's earlier acknowledgment of the Miltonic "sylvan scene" almost unnecessary.

About the reciprocating, compensatory song of the hermit thrush—in the part that Eliot himself, in 1923 at least, thought more highly of than any other in the poem—one can only conjecture. The "sound of water over a rock / Where the hermit-thrush sings in the pine trees" (lines 355–56) is glossed in the notes with a quotation from an ornithological handbook, but it may come as well "from deep secluded recesses, / From the fragrant cedars and the ghostly pines so still" of another major text. "Solitary the thrush, / The hermit withdrawn to himself. . . ." of "When Lilacs Last in the Dooryard Bloom'd" may be making a reappearance in another poem in which sexuality and loss are strangely involved. Whitman had transcended the trope of funerary roses and lilies with his erotic lilac branch, and in Eliot's hyacinth poem, the hermit thrush (perhaps, too, returning so beautifully in "Marina" in another carol of death) may partake of that bird's modern mythography as well as of its acoustical presence. The associations of the hermit thrush with the Tristan legend, which the poetess Adelaide Crapsey explored in a cinquain,[14] may perhaps also have been at work in *The Waste Land*'s range of fable. It is at any rate worthy of note here that the song of the thrush itself (*The Waste Land,* line 358): "Drip drop drip drop drop drop drop" modulates from the conventionalized "drip drop" of water to the "drop drop drop drop" ("Like melting snow upon some craggie hill") of the beautiful song sung by none other than Echo in Ben Jonson's *Cynthia's Revels,* in which echo, water, rock, and lamentation for loss all come together. But the extremely complex allusive and echoing texture of the whole poem may need some future study in the rhetoric of acknowledgment, and of the ways in which scholia of citation enter into poetic texts themselves.[15]

14. Adelaide Crapsey's cinquain was written before 1914, but only published in 1934. See her *Complete Poems and Collected Letters,* ed. Susan S. Smith (Albany, 1977), 103. Not only the hermit thrush echoes Whitman: the "third who always walks beside you" may very well go back to lines 120–25 of "When Lilacs Last in the Dooryard Bloom'd."

15. S. Musgrove, in *T.S. Eliot and Walt Whitman* (Wellington, 1952) made no distinction between echo and allusion in pointing out the presence of Whitman in Eliot's poems. Following his study, subsequent essays by himself and W.K. Wimsatt on Eliot and Tennyson, and R.F. Fleissner, D.J. DeLaura, and others on Eliot and Pater, the echoing of texts whose manifest presence seems otherwise to be evaded or denied in Eliot's work

A common source of echo in twentieth-century literature will be recognized in the allusive titling of novels. The artfully carved-out fragment of quotation—biblical, Shakespearean, or whatever—summons up its context with an evocative power: *"Measure for Measure"* is a good early example, as is *"The Sound and the Fury"* a later one. We might say that in order to understand the title, its relation to the work, and thereby something about the work itself, the fragment of quoted material must be traced to its source. Ultimately, we should have in the first case to restore the verse from the Sermon on the Mount, and indeed, its antecedent ("Judge not, that ye be not judged" Matthew 7:1–2), in order to "read" the title properly, and thereby to assess its role and genre of titling. Likewise, the suppressed half of the quoted line from *Macbeth* (from a passage that has yielded more than a fair share of allusive titles), *"Told by an idiot,* full of sound and fury" (italics added), points to Faulkner's making the visionary idiot Benjy a significant narrator. In these instances, the titles implicitly assume a reader's knowledge of the source. Thereby, they remain instances of allusion, rather than of echo.[16]

I could imagine true echo creeping into an allusive title only when something has gone wrong—some trick of memory or misconstruction—with the process of alluding. An easy example is the title of the popular antebellum fan-

---

now seems obvious. I would add to the scholia at this point only a suggestion that the "History is now and England" of "Little Gidding" ironically, and perhaps unwittingly, reworks Pater in *Marius the Epicurean: "America is here and how: here or nowhere:* as Wilhelm Meister finds out one day, just not too late, after so long looking vaguely across the ocean for the opportunity of the development of his capacities."

16. But not in the case of the title of Thomas Hardy's great lyric, "During Wind and Rain," with its echo of the refrain of Feste's song in *Twelfth Night;* Hardy's poem enacts a revision of the earlier song's synoptic narrative punctuated by natural recurrence.

tasy, *Gone with the Wind*. The implicit grammar of the phrase, in relation to the book's subject, suggests that the Old South has "gone"—vanished—along with the passing wind, and to wherever the winds go. But in the context of its source, Ernest Dowson's poem about Cynara, the phrase has a different syntax, and a different sense:

> I have forgot much, Cynara! gone with the wind,
> Flung roses, roses riotously with the throng,
> Dancing to put thy pale, lost lilies out of mind. . . .

Here, *forgot, gone,* and *flung* are all compound and parallel, and the subject of all of them is *I* (have); *gone* means "run," "gone to play," not "vanished." But perhaps the American title's misreading of the syntax was abetted by another resonant memory (aside from the association of "pale, lost lilies" with the faded belles of the story). Although there is no trace of verbal echo, the missing presence may come at the end of the phrase, "gone with the wind—*like the ghosts of leaves from an enchanter fleeing*"; and Shelley's west wind of destruction and preservation may be blowing through the mistake. Even the milieu of Dowson's phrase brings up a matter of erotic loss, and perhaps the peculiarities of her title, which create a new meaning and resonance for the phrase as if Dowson had never written, must be deemed Miss Mitchell's major literary accomplishment. (It is amusing to speculate on a prior echo of Dowson's phrase: "Gone with the wind. Hosts at Mullaghmast and Tara of the kings." This is from the "Aeolus" chapter of *Ulysses;*[17] the fragmentation of the interior monologue avoids a direct syntactic decision in the text of the echo, but the effect is clearly like that of Mitchell's revision. Stephen Dedalus' association of Dowson's wind with the vanished Tara, in a context, in *Ulysses,* of rhetorical hot air, seems uncannily

17. James Joyce, *Ulysses* (New York, 1961), 143.

like a notebook germ of Miss Mitchell's book. I doubt that it was.)

Echoes can be so faint and fragmentary that they seem to enter a poem as tonal quality, or shading of voice, even as harmonic partials, accompanying a fundamental pitch, enter and shape its world of timbre rather than being heard in their own right. Walter Savage Landor's magnificent and heartbreaking poem about an old man's relation to fading memory is manifestly concerned with traces, fragments, and losses of language. I cannot resist quoting this masterpiece, "Memory", entire:

> The Mother of the Muses, we are taught,
> Is Memory: she has left me; they remain,
> And shake my shoulder, urging me to sing
> About the summer days, my loves of old.
> *Alas! alas!* is all I can reply.
> Memory has left with me that name alone,
> Harmonious name, which other bards may sing,
> But her bright image in my darkest hour
> Comes back, in vain comes back, called or uncalled.
> Forgotten are the names of visitors
> Ready to press my hand but yesterday;
> Forgotten are the names of earlier friends
> Whose genial converse and glad countenance
> Are fresh as ever to mine ear and eye;
> To these, when I have written and besought
> Remembrance of me, the word *Dear* alone
> Hangs on the upper verge, and waits in vain.
> A blessing wert thou, O oblivion,
> If thy stream carried only weeds away,
> But vernal and autumnal flowers alike
> It hurries down to wither on the strand.

Memory departs like the body of the nymph of Echo, leaving only the name of a poetical beloved, "harmonious name"—Miltonic name, and lines 7–9 ring with fragments of the invocations to Books III, VII, and IX of *Paradise Lost*. Loss of memory is covertly likened to a blindness, even though remembering is summoned up by "thoughts that voluntary move / Harmonious numbers; as the wakeful Bird / Sings darkling" (III, 37–39); Landor, too, is "fall'n on evil days, / on evil days though fall'n and evil tongues; / In darkness, and with dangers compast round" (VII, 25–27), although these dangers and evils and darknesses are occasioned by the occlusion of light from the past. Memory herself is no muse, as Landor must have remembered writing in a poem to Wordsworth years earlier. But her empty personification is an ironic dark shadow of the presence of Milton's "Celestial Patronness who deigns / Her nightly visitation unimplor'd, / And dictates to me slumb'ring" (IX, 21–23)." These passages resonate vaguely, but confusedly, in Landor's lines, and account for their Miltonic flavor. More important, these passages provide the cave of resonance—the context of the evocative blindness or darkness—which enables Landor to remember enough to write his poem of forgetting, of loss of precision and identity (he can only write to beloved friends, "Dear X or Y"). We might say that, indeed, his muse is still there because without realizing it, he can still "remember" cadences and echoes of Milton.

The concept of source, although derived from the poetic mythology of fountains, is polytopical, covering commonplaces as well as specific loci of quotation, allusion, and echo. Very often these may compete for the ear of the overhearer in a given poetic place. Various "sources" for the penultimate image of Andrew Marvell's "Coy Mistress" poem have been suggested. Thus, "And tear our pleasures with rough strife / Thorough the iron gates of life" may be an implicit contrastive ("through the Iron Gates of *life,* as opposed to the famous gates on the Danube," or even "through the *iron* gates—as opposed to horn or ivory—of

life, which fractures and transcends dreaming"). It may, as
has been suggested[18] allude to Spenser's Garden of Adonis
in *The Faerie Queene* (III. vi. 31), sited "in fruitfull soyle of
old,"

> And girt in with two walls on either side,
> The one of yron, the other of bright gold,
> That none might thorough breake, nor overstride;
> And double gates it had, which opened wide . . .

In this case, the "iron gates" would have been assembled
from different lines. But if this is a true echo, it might account for the less than usual "thorough" for *through* in Marvell's line. The echo may be indeed more direct, however,
and from Shakespeare. If so, the "rough strife" of actual
flesh and metaphorical iron finds a complementary anterior
milieu:

> "For stones dissolv'd to water do convert.
> O, if no harder than a stone thou art,
>   Melt at my tears and be compassionate!
>   Soft pity enters at an iron gate."

implores Lucrece of Tarquin (*The Rape of Lucrece,* 592–95),
but of course to no avail. In either of these instances, the
image of the iron gates would have a different kind of referential background from those in the two contrastive situations proposed first.

A somewhat different version of this situation occurs
when a later poem may be echoing either or both of two
earlier ones, but where the relation between the two earlier
texts is itself clearly resonant. Tennyson's *The Passing of
Arthur* concludes with Sir Bedivere climbing to a height to
watch for the last possible trace of Arthur's body being
borne across the water,

18. J. E. Hankins, in *Source and Meaning in Spenser's Allegory* (Oxford,
1971), 268.

> . . . and saw,
> Straining his eyes beneath an arch of hand,
> Or thought he saw, the speck that bare the King. (lines 463–65)

An ultimate locus may be Aeneas seeing the dim form of Dido amid shadows in Book VI of the *Aeneid* (line 454), "even as early in the month one sees, or thinks he has seen [*aut videt aut vidisse putat*] the moon rise amid clouds." The recollection of this is important at the end of *Paradise Lost,* Book I, when the apparent grandeur of the demonic conclave is being shaded by simile, and there are introduced elves,

> Whose midnight Revels, by a forest side
> Or Fountain some belated Peasant sees
> Or dreams he sees, while overhead the Moon
> Sits Arbitress. . . .   (lines 782–85)

Tennyson echoes Milton's melody; although the echo is softened by the interposed modifying line, the pattern "sees / Or dreams he sees" is answered in "saw / Or thought he saw." On the other hand, it is Milton who responds to the resonating ambiance in Virgil, the presence of the moon. Perhaps if Tennyson were, at one level of intention, to be recalling the Virgil he knew so well, some inner ear was at the same time summoning up the canonical version of that Virgilian moment in English. In this case, Milton's echo is more significant, though muffled structurally and rhythmically by translation; Tennyson's resounds more clearly, but with less rich a meaning.

The rebounds of intertextual echo generally, then, distort the original voice in order to interpret it. From the chopping-off or fragmentation of the echo device within texts as studied in the previous chapter, to the more subtly modified revisions of allusion, the figure that has come to replace the nymph of mythology responds in many tones. It is no longer even a matter of choosing between a derisive, mocking echo, attenuated by an uncompletable attachment to Narcissus, and a more mysterious, affirming, harmonizing echo, the rumored consort of Pan. Allusive echo inhabits a figurative realm which is not that of the ironist, or the synecdochist, alone, but rather one which seems itself to comment on these. I shall draw a tentative map of that realm in the next chapter.

V.
Echo Metaleptic

Implicit in the previous discussions has been the treatment of allusive echo, leading from poem to poem, as being itself a trope of the later text. But rhetoric, like many theories of signification, is a synchronic study; what we seem to have been considering is a sort of diachronic figure. Any kind of wordplay, of allusion to other meanings or homonyms of a word, is usually thought of as linking references in some kind of conceptual space, and a time-frame is never considered. In Spenserian narrative, a sort of visionary linguistics sets up a scheme within which the history of the reader's acquaintance with a word or morpheme (usually a name) may be operative. Thus, in Book I of *The Faerie Queene,* the final syllables of the name of *Fidessa* read, on our first aquaintance with the lady, as a delicate feminine substantive ending, personifying the faith and trust of *fides.* The unveiling of that whorish consort of Archimago is also the dissolution of a folk etymology: the final syllables are really those of *Duessa* (doubleness as falsehood—as in *due + esse*), whose name had been introduced, as that of some sorceress, some eight stanzas later in the second canto.

But it is *Paradise Lost* that introduces diachronic semantics—in the earlier and derived meanings of words—as a trope of the fallen and unfallen conditions. Major English and American poetry after Milton would continue to play on the relation between a "present," contemporary meaning of a word, and an alluded-to, earlier, "original" one—a dialectic of the prior as opposed to the phenomenologically primary. Prior meanings are not prior texts, but a figurative use of language which engages them locates one

kind of poetic activity in the panchronic situation which
Saussure denied to analysis.[1] In short, we deal with diachronic trope all the time, and yet we have no name for it as
a class. An echo of the kind we have been considering may
occur in a figure in a poem, and it may echo the language of a
figure in a previous one. But the echoing itself makes a
figure, and the interpretive or revisionary power which
raises the echo even louder than the original voice is that of a
trope of diachrony.

I propose that we apply the name of the classical rhetoricians' trope of *transumption* (or *metalepsis,* in its Greek form)
to these diachronic, allusive figures. Quintilian identified
transumption as a movement from one trope to another,
which operates through one or more middle terms of
figuration.[2] Subsequent rhetoricians, from St. Augustine
through the English Renaissance critic George Puttenham
(who refers to it as the trope of the far-fetched) are in confused disagreement about its function. It can be the effect for
the cause, the subsequent for the antecedent, the late for the
early, for example, but there is a general sense that it is a kind
of meta-trope, or figure of linkage between figures, and that
there will be one or more unstated middle terms which are
leapt over, or alluded to, by the figure. A synchronic treatment of metalepsis—of a trope of a trope, as it were—might
merely be a *catachresis,* or thoroughly mixed metaphor. But
in a highly allusive situation, in which an image or fable is
being presented as a revision of an earlier one, the diachrony
is inescapable.

Consider for a moment the peculiar quality of Miltonic
simile, by which, as Dr. Johnson put it, Milton "crowds the

1. F. de Saussure, *Cours de linguistique générale,* III, 5–7.

2. See the Appendix for the history of the terms *metalepsis* and *transumption* from Quintilian on. Harold Bloom, in *A Map of Misreading* (New
York, 1975) appropriated it as the name for his ultimate trope of revision,
following Fletcher (see note 4 below).

imagination," as a mode of transumption. The very multi-tudinousness of the Satanic legions in Book I, lines 301–4 of *Paradise Lost* is like that of autumn leaves, and the simile claims this manifestly as the basis of the comparison. Unstated, suppressed, however, are the other likenesses (both leaves and rebel armies are fallen, and dead) whose presence is shadowed only in the literalizing of the place name of *Vallombrosa*.

Miltonic simile is now generally understood as a form which likens A to B *in that* X is palpably true of them both, but with no mention of W, Y, and Z, which are also true of them both. As a heuristic fiction, the simile will eventually call on the reader to consider the unmentioned W, Y, Z, or whatever. It will also ask why these, frequently more significant or pressing, should seem less immediately apparent than X; and what this implies about the relations among the predicates (W, X, Y, Z), and the distance between the A and B that are likened with respect to them. Similes are expository figures, not tropes, but Milton's are clearly tropes. It is in the transumption of the W, Y, Z, etc., that an expository structure gains figurative force. (Likewise metaleptic in Milton are the connections between similes or comparisons, covered by the innocently disjunctive-looking *or* (surely a Latin *vel* rather than an *aut* in any case).

Proper reading of a metaphor demands a simultaneous appreciation of the beauty of the vehicle and of the importance of its freight (with perhaps a sense of the higher beauty of the appropriateness of the very mode of transportation). But the interpretation of a metalepsis entails the recovery of the transumed material. A transumptive style is to be distinguished radically from the kind of conceited one that we usually associate with baroque poetic, and with English seventeenth-century verse in particular. It involves an ellipsis, rather than a relentless pursuit, of further figuration. As a clearly delineated class of trope, metalepsis seems both elusive and allusive at once. It is with respect to this allusiveness that further complications arise.

We have been considering the figure synchronically only, but it is clear that certain kinds of allusion are in themselves transumptive. A Renaissance writer citing a classical myth, for example, may very well be doing so with respect to a specific moralization or other interpretation of the personage or event. Thus, Milton invokes Bellerophon falling from Pegasus onto a plain whose name he makes sound like a word for error or wandering. But the metalepsis in that invocation to *Paradise Lost* Book VII is of the reading of the story of Bellerophon on Pegasus killing the Chimera as a case of poetry—rather than philosophy—killing falsehood. (There may be an additional incorporation of the mythographer Conti's report that Bellerophon ended up blind, as well.)

It is also possible that some of the problems of relating rhetorical to iconographic concepts in Renaissance imagery—the questions raised by scholars such as Praz, D.J. Gordon, Gombrich, and others—have a metaleptic dimension. Consider, for example, a line in the lovely lyric about retirement that was formerly ascribed to George Peele (it is probably by Sir Henry Lee), and is entitled in anthologies "A Farewell to Arms for Queen Elizabeth." It begins, "His golden locks Time hath to silver turned." The line in question starts off the second stanza: "His helmet now shall make a hive for bees"—a parallel to the biblical "swords into ploughshares." But the image preexists the poem. It can be found in Geoffrey Whitney's *Choise of Emblemes* as a picture of "Ex Bello, Pax" and, perhaps, in other iconographic sources. One way of characterizing the elusive relation of picture to complex metaphor might be to say that there had been a transumption of the emblem, as opposed to an outright allusion, e.g., "His sword into a ploughshare Time has wrought." Or suppose, "His helmet now is turned to the proverbial hive" (with *proverbial* a *hypallage* modifying *helmet,* in Latinate fashion, as well): we would tend to feel less figurative force in the first of these alternatives, and even less in the second. Perhaps the original line is indeed metaleptic of the picture. Or perhaps it is only a matter of not so common a commonplace being recalled.[3]

In any event, we are back in the realm of allusion. Perhaps the association is inevitable. Angus Fletcher first called modern critical attention to metalepsis in a discussive footnote, in his *Allegory,* on Milton's allusiveness, and on Samuel Johnson's reminder that "he saw nature, as Dryden expresses it, *through the spectacles of books.*"[4] In the following paragraph, Johnson talks of Milton's similes and of the imaginative crowding in the comparison of Satan's shield to the moon seen through Galileo's telescope. The sequence of similes that extends from that of the moon, through the two comparisons of the legions of fallen angels, to the autumn leaves and the sedge, has been studied by Geoffrey Hartman[5] for just this effect of packing and connecting. Overlooked generally in such discussions is the matter of Satan's spear. The poetic handling of it has traditionally seemed a moment of respite in the unfolding of what Dr. Johnson calls the characteristic "amplitude." Here are the lines in question:

> His spear, to equal which the tallest Pine
> Hewn on Norwegian hills, to be the Mast
> Of some great Ammiral, were but a wand,
> He walked with to support uneasy steps
> Over the burning Marl . . .   (I, 292–96)

3. Leo Steinberg has written elegantly and profoundly about modes of pictorial allusiveness that seem metaleptic and revisionary; see "Pontormo's Capponi Chapel," *Art Bulletin* 56 (1974), especially pp. 396–98.

4. Angus Fletcher, *Allegory* (Ithaca, 1964), 241n.

5. Geoffrey Hartman, "Milton's Counterplot," in *Beyond Formalism* (New Haven, 1970), 113–23.

On the face of it, the simple comparison to the magnitude of the pine has none of the allusive pregnancy of the surrounding similes. The scale of a mainmast for the hugeness of the spear originates with Homer: Polyphemus' club "being an Olive tree / Which late he feld"—as Chapman gives it—was "so vast / That we resembl'd it to some fit Mast / To serve a ship of burthen that was driven / With twentie Oares. . . ." (*Odyssey* IX, 445–48). Tasso, in Fairfax's translation (*Jerusalem Delivered* VI, 40), tells us that Tancred and Argantes "bore, instead of spears, / Two knotty masts, which none but they could lift." Our first interpretive impulse would be to treat Satan's spear as a borrowing of Polyphemus'.

In that case, Milton would be merely doing what Tasso did or, more particularly, what Abraham Cowley did. In his biblical epic *Davideis,* Cowley (perhaps thinking of Sylvester's translation of Du Bartas, *The Divine Weeks and Works*) describes Goliath thus: "His *Spear* the *Trunk* was of a lofty *Tree* / Which *Nature* meant some tall *Ship's Mast* to be" (III, 393–94). Cowley, in his notes to his own poem, calls attention to these lines. But all he seems concerned with is the possible hyperbole in them, not citing Homer, but noting that he had himself written earlier "Th'*Egyptian* like an Hill himself did rear; / Like some tall Tree upon it stood his Spear." All Cowley can see in his conflation of predecessors (Virgil, Ovid, Du Bartas) is authority for a picturesque figure. His citation of them is of the allusive sort that pervades so much translated near-echo from classical texts: there is no resonance of context. Milton, however, conscious of Cowley and others behind him, is an experienced reader of allusive lines that are innocent of deeper figurative intention. When he alludes, it will be with a transumptive version of allusion itself.

For Satan is not to be linked only—and momentarily—

with Goliath. A third huge figure, walking with an actual pine (rather than something bigger) "to support uneasy steps" comes classically to mind. It is that of Polyphemus in the *Aeneid* (III, 559): "trunca manu pinus regit et vestigia firmat" ("in his hand a lopped pine guides and steadies his steps"). Perhaps a shadow more than actual verbal echo, the literally blind Polyphemus figures the metaphorically blind Satan. Moreover, the whole Virgilian topos was so sensitive for Milton that it was bound to resonate for him; the preceding line in the *Aeneid* describes Polyphemus as "monstrum horrendum, informe, ingens, cui lumen ademptum" ("a horrid monster, shapeless, huge, bereft of light"). It was just this line that was hurled, as a polemical spear, at Milton by the author of the *Cry of the Royal Blood* pamphlet (1652), which evoked Milton's *Second Defense.* Milton reacted polemically to the use of the line there and in the *Defensio pro se;* it is hard to believe that he did not remember it later on. In *Paradise Lost,* it is almost like a silent echo accompanying the loud machinery of merely physical comparison.

That Satan's spear occupies an allusively charged—or as Dr. Johnson put it, imaginatively crowded—region of *Paradise Lost* was understood by Pope, who must have overheard the many echoes.[6] In his own translation of Homer's lines on the death of Sarpedon, in a totally different context (*Iliad* XVI, 591–95), he gives: "Then, as the mountain Oak, or Poplar tall / Or pine (fit mast for some great Admiral) / Nods to the Ax . . . Thus fell the King." Pope echoes Milton's "to be the Mast / Of some great Ammiral," but with a wonderfully resonant misprision of it. Milton's word *Ammiral* is not, in this context, the metonymy that it is in

6. Some aspects of Pope's use of Milton in dealing with Homer have been noted by Douglas Knight, *Pope and the Heroic Tradition* (New Haven, 1951), 53–60.

Pope's case (the mast of some great admiral's ship); rather, Milton is using the Italian sense, *ammiraglia* or "flagship." Pope seems to be calling attention to the person of the Admiral, the commander, as parallel to the King (Sarpedon).

With Pope's echo, a final tone of Milton's is amplified. In transcending the mast-comparison in size ("the tallest Pine . . . Ammiral, *were but a wand*" [italics added]) he is also therein transcending the prior allusions, even as he has alluded to them. It is like a summing up of the range of texts for him, tempting us to play with the notion of transumption as if the Latin word were a portmanteau of transcending and summing up over, in the mathematical sense.

And finally there is the matter of the pine tree itself. The Homeric mast could be an olive tree, but the Virgilian one was taller yet; Milton's is not only taller yet again, but richer. Milton—and often, as we have begun to realize, Spenser—seems as incapable of making a passive move, of writing merely narrative or expository filler, as James Joyce. The comparison to the pine is itself allusive. In describing the Golden Age, Ovid (*Metamorphoses* I, 94–95) says that "nondum caesa suis, peregrinum ut viseret orbem / montibus in liquidas pinus descenderat undas" (in George Sandys' version, "To visit other worlds no wounded pine / Did yet from hills to faithless seas decline"). Satan's spear reeks of implicit technology: it is almost as if he had, by uprooting the otherwise patient pine, torn up the Golden Age. Sandys in his commentary on this passage links the Age with Paradise ("Saturne was throwne out of Heaven, and Adam out of Paradice," and "Saturne was the first that invented tillage, and so was Adam. . . .") Having retrieved the allusion, we can see *why* the spear is likened to an actual kind of tall pine: there is a transumption of its mythology.

The famous image following that of the spear in Milton's chain of similes at this point in Book I reveals another instance of this kind of allusiveness:

> he stood and call'd
> His Legions, Angel Forms, who lay intrans't
> Thick as Autumnal Leaves that strow the Brooks
> In *Vallombrosa,* where th' *Etrurian* shades
> High overarch't imbow'r. . . .   (lines 300–4)

The fallen leaves, themselves full of Homeric, Virgilian, and Dantesque associations, bring together tropes of death, multitudinousness, falling and scattered generational and Sybilline leaves, and so forth. By the time the image has moved through Shelley's "yellow, and black, and pale, and hectic red, / Pestilence-stricken multitudes," through the echoing line in Hardy's "During Wind and Rain" ("How the sick leaves reel down in throngs!"), to Allen Tate's refrain in the "Ode for the Confederate Dead," the problem is almost that of a topos.[7]

Certainly, as Harold Bloom has shown,[8] the turning of the leaves in the wind in Stevens' "Domination of Black" is an allusive and transumptive (in the senses he has given to the word) image; it has added Whitman's leaves = blades + pages (as Stevens adopts the *of* of Whitman's title—"about" and "composed of"—in so many of his ambiguous genitive constructions). The "turning" is of pages, as well as of autumnal coloring, and the Sibylline component of the trope becomes reconstituted through the presence of Whitman. (It is even possible that the suppression of all mention of black in the poem itself may be related to a suppression of any trace of the "black leaves wheeling in the wind" from Oscar Wilde's immensely corny "The Harlot's House.") For Stevens, the image of the leaves, revising itself in the firelight of imagination, is like "the leaves themselves, / Turning in the wind." Like songbirds that stand for

7. So Vladimir, in *Waiting for Godot,* Act I, seems to imply, in his insistence on what the voices of the dead sound like.
8. Harold Bloom, *Wallace Stevens: The Poems of Our Climate* (Ithaca, 1977), 58–81, 375–79, and passim.

more than the natural noises they produce, summing up over the range of nightingales and skylarks behind them (e.g., Hardy's thrush), the trope of the leaves is metaleptic, rather than merely metaphoric. Its allusiveness has been brought into the range of its subject. It is almost as if for us, now, the image "means," among other things: "Even as leaves turn color and die, and the Sybil's scattered leaves are reconstituted metaphorically in all our own writings— whoever we are, and whenever we write—even as men fall like leaves, and become mulch for new generations, even as the leaves of the book of life turn, so does the very image of fallen leaves present itself for revision."

Miltonic similes and classical allusions are frequently metaleptic in this manner, but so is much modern imagery. Sometimes this is programmatically obvious:

> The rose is obsolete
> but each petal ends in
> an edge, the double facet
> cementing the grooved
> columns of air—The edge
> cuts without cutting

William Carlos Williams, in *Spring and All VII,* is proclaiming a modernist transumption of the "obsolete" trope of roses. With brilliant punning on two senses of *end* (a synonym for "edge," and "terminus"), he moves the problem into the realm of visual representation, and alludes to the challenge to painting of Cézanne's revision of the relation between objects and the space around them. The latest rebirth of pictorial space becomes for Williams a trope for the rebirth of trope itself; and cubism becomes, momentarily, modern poetry.

Sometimes the transumptive quality of a moment will be as haunting—as elusively allusive—as a faint but actual verbal echo. Whitman's beautiful fable of the moon becoming moonlight in order to make love to the twenty-eight days, the young men swimming in the ocean, seems strangely evocative when the lunar woman is described: "She owns the fine house by the rise of the bank, / She hides handsome and richly drest aft the blinds of the window" (*Song of Myself* 11, 4–5). A context of erotic danger for young men is provided by the famous parable of the harlot, Proverbs 7:6–27, beginning "for at the window of my house I looked through the casement, and beheld among the simple ones, I discerned among the youths, a young man void of understanding . . . in the twilight, in the evening, in the black and dark night." Whitman clearly identifies himself with the twenty-eight-year-old moon woman behind the blinds, and the separation of narrator and harlot in the biblical passage is reconstituted in his figure of the watcher.

Whether or not Whitman's passage partakes of the biblical text, however, it nevertheless undergoes a beautiful transumption in the first of Hart Crane's "Voyages" poems. There, the young men become the "bright striped urchins" whom the poet is warning away from engulfing sexual experience ("The bottom of the sea is cruel"). The moon-woman-Whitman becomes the purely female sea, whose bottom is sexual and dangerous, and the poet stands aside to observe and to caution. It is significant that when he does so, the tone echoes Whitman so clearly, in "and could they hear me I would tell them: // O brilliant kids, frisk with your dog, / Fondle your shells and your sticks. . . ." The particular way in which Crane's scene alludes to Whitman's, including the relation of the "I" of his poem to that of the earlier one, is like a scenic echo, or shadow.

Often, when an image, or system of images, is itself the object of a later allusive transumption, there can be true interpretive mystery. This is particularly the case when a commonplace is being engaged and when, as in chains of echoes—or in a manuscript stemma, for that matter—there is a question of a common or intermediate source. To speak of the woods in *A Maske Presented at Ludlow Castle* as a transumption of Dante's *selva oscura,* Spenser's forest of "Errour," and so forth, invokes no problematic allusion. But what about the accidental historical relation of young Alice Egerton (as the Lady) in the woods of Milton's masque, and Alice Liddell (as Alice) in the wood in *Through the Looking Glass?* She wanders through the woods in which everyone forgets his or her or its name "with her arms clasped lovingly around the neck of the fawn" (making up a Spenserian emblem of Lady and Creature, and more significantly comprising the only moment of physical tenderness that I can recall in the *Alice* books). Is she simply straying into an accident of interpretation?

Such problems point to an aspect of reading heavily metaleptic texts that has its analogies in the interpretation of graphic collage in modern art. There, a major dimension of form and signification is the interplay of recognizable *source* and that source's surrender to immediate local and overall pictorial *role.* Collage and elements of it in analytic cubist painting represent a kind of schematic medium for the study of pictorial intertextuality. The study of this medium could lead to an understanding of the metamorphosis of graphic image as a step beyond the metamorphosis of human or animal or objective form. More than these satirical transformations (such as those of Circe or any Aesopian magician), the metamorphosis of image or graphic convention comments on the operations of consciousness itself. Hegel's characterization of mythological composites—gods, monsters, etc.—moralized as fables of mind (or, perhaps, as fables of trope or fable itself) suggests itself here. He speaks of composites wherein the animal's shape

at the same time is one which is superseded [*aufgehoben*] and becomes the hieroglyphic symbol of another meaning, the hieroglyph of a thought. Hence also this shape is no longer solely and entirely used by the worker, but becomes blended with the shape embodying thought, with the human form.[9]

as if the composite form were itself an emblem of the emblematized, of myth *cum* interpretation.

   Notwithstanding the distinction I have been making between allusion and echo, it must be said that there are distinctly metaleptic kinds of allusion that are clearly not echoes, and I should refer readers at once to studies of *symboliste* imagery for more on this.[10] Then, too, there is a mode of apparent allusion to actuality, rather than to text, which must be nonetheless clearly distinguished from merely exotic or abstruse or even metaphysically conceited figures. In Robert Frost's sonnet "The Silken Tent" we get the initially puzzling "when a sunny summer breeze / Has dried the dew and all its ropes relent"—puzzling because we should expect dry ropes to contract on drying, rather than to expand and "relent." But the mistake, and its correction, are themselves part of the meditation in which the poem invites us to participate: braided ropes (as in guy ropes or rigging) when wet expand across their diameters, and consequently contract along their lengths. When we think otherwise, we are confusing ropes that support and control with, say, leather thongs which constrain. Since the poem explores one aspect of the relation between contingency and freedom, the image is a potent one; its power seems to depend upon allusion to fact, rather than to the drawing out of detail (imagine the garrulous, almost Cowleyan mode in

   9. G. W. F. Hegel, *The Phenomenology of Mind,* tr. J. B. Baillie (London, 1931), 706.
   10. James Kugel, *The Techniques of Strangeness in Symbolist Poetry* (New Haven, 1971), 32–50, is relevant here with his remarks on what he calls "frustrated allusion." I suppose that a theorist of revision like Harold Bloom would argue that all textual echoing is the *Nachklang* of "belatedness," of which condition he might cite *symbolisme* itself as an instance.

which Browning, for example, might have handled the matter of the rope's expansion).

I should guess, however, that any systematic reader of Frost's poetry might be able to show the textually allusive quality of the "thrush music" in "Come In." Versions of tropes, "turnings" of them, are in this sense tropes of tropes, (as Quintilian called them, whatever he may have meant).[11] The "grimy scraps / Of withered leaves about your feet / And newspapers from vacant lots" of Eliot's "Preludes" are transumptive in this way, and in addition have contributed to the iconography of the newspaper blown down vacant streets, an emblem of urban desolation. Another such transumptively allusive figure manifests a revaluation as well. Again from Hart Crane ("Cape Hatteras"):

> New verities, new inklings in the velvet hummed
> Of dynamos, where hearing's leash is strummed . . .
> Power's script,—wound, bobbin-bound, refined—
> Is stropped to the slap of belts on booming spools, spurred
> Into the bulging bouillon, harnessed jelly of the stars.

The immediate verbal echo—"wound, bobbin-bound"—is Yeatsian; the major metalepsis, however, is of Blake (*Jerusalem,* Plate 15), crying out against "the Schools and Universities of Europe," with "the Loom of Locke" and the "water-wheels of Newton":

> cruel Works
> Of many Wheels I view, wheel without wheel, with cogs tyrannic
> Moving by compulsion each other: not as those in Eden: which
> Wheel within Wheel in freedom revolve in harmony & peace.
>
> (lines 17–20)

These "dark Satanic wheels" (*Jerusalem,* 11, 44), themselves carrying a verbal echo of the "dark Satanic mills" of the prefatory lyric to *Milton,* are gears, moving each other by a

11. See the Appendix for a discussion of this.

mechanical and deterministic compulsion, as opposed to the visionary fluid drive of the Ezekiel-like wheels in Eden. Crane, following the reconstitution of technological progress as possible spiritual development envisioned in Whitman's *Passage to India,* makes a spiritual trope of belt-driven machinery. Its connections to the perceiver are stressed ("hearing's leash is strummed"). The "new verities" are metaleptic of the old truths of compulsion; Crane has made belts turn spools with the freedom and promise of wheels within wheels.

The only schematic trace of Blake in Crane's lines is in the last one quoted, the rhythm of the blank fourteener Blake uses throughout the long poems. Crane's iambic pentameters, whether rhymed or blank, are frequently varied with hypermetrical lines, usually a form of alexandrine. In the lines above, he moves into the sort of expressionist variation he sometimes employs in various parts of *The Bridge,* but the final fourteener is almost unique, and echoes Blake in its movement. Yeats too had written of Locke and bobbins and the spinning jenny, and Crane reels off additional figurative force from Yeats' bobbin. Yet the allusive image probably goes back directly to Blake, and makes us almost want to speak of the transumption of the machine itself—as Whitman says somewhere, "Echoes of things, reverberant, an aftermath." But perhaps always accompanied, somewhere, by poetic *Nachklang.*

I conclude these observations on the metaleptic nature of poetic echo with a final note on two aspects of reechoing. The first has been observed earlier in passing: texts themselves in manifesting schematic repetition or self-echo can be particularly resonant when picked up allusively later on. The reflexive pattern of the first line of Milton's *Lycidas,* "Yet once more, O ye Laurels, and once more" (considered for a moment in isolation from the enjambed second one:

"Ye myrtles brown. . . .") reverberates with belatedness. Aside from its own miniature echo device, it allusively echoes a passage in the King James translation of Hebrews 12:26–27, whose own "yet once more" probably itself echoes an original one in Haggai 2:6. Louis Martz has eloquently commented upon Milton's relation to the Pauline passage; we might only notice here that the biblical text itself has a transumptive flavor: "Whose voice then shook the earth: but now he hath promised, saying, Yet once more I shake not the earth only, but also Heaven. And this word, Yet once more, signifying the removing of those things that are shaken, as of things that are made, that those things which cannot be shaken may remain." Milton's metaleptic echo involves other versions of shaking and of what may remain (berries? poetic fruit?). It is itself a case of "yet once more and once more a 'yet once more,'" allusive of the youngish poet's own previous elegiac poems, of pastoral elegiac tradition, perhaps even half-wittingly of Spenser's massive revisions of pastoral and of the major lyrical poem. To all of these *Lycidas* holds a transumptive relationship.[12]

The beautifully talented young American poet Trumbull Stickney, writing in 1898 near the Tyrol (far from Miltonic or Shelleyan Tuscan ground) begins his ode "In Ampezzo" with a delicate transumptive version of Milton's opening:

> Only once more and not again—the larches
> Shake to the wind their echo, "Not again,"—
> We see, below the sky that over-arches
> Heavy and blue, the plain

12. This is particularly noticeable at the end of the poem, where the "mantle blue" of the uncouth swain can, syntactically, be associated with the sun as well, and where, in any case, the "And now" revises Spenser's "and nowe the frosty Night / Her mantle black through heaven gan over-haile," at the end of the "January" eclogue of *The Shepheardes Calender*. This is an end that is also at a beginning: the transumption is not only of Night's black for the youthful sun's blue, but of *Lycidas* for Spenser's pastoral generally.

Stickney, an excellent Greek scholar, may be specifically hearing the New Testament Greek behind Milton's English "yet once more"—*eti hapax,* ("once and for all"). He is certainly attentive to the fallen leaves passage in *Paradise Lost* considered a few pages back ("Where th' Etrurian shades / High overarch't imbow'r"). This is a late, sad shaking and echoing, and a late revision both of a visionary moment and a poetic mode of self-conscious recapitulation. The echo scheme, allusively echoing an earlier allusive echo scheme: both of these generated originally by a biblical "yet once more" and its repetition in the canonical mode of the interpreter.[13]

A final instance of an interpretive transumption involves a whole prior tradition of the poetic treatment of echo. The actual allusive echo in the famous song about echoes, beginning "The splendour falls on castle walls," from Tennyson's *The Princess,* is rather faint: the Spenserian alexandrine of the last refrain, "Blow bugle blow, set the wild echoes flying, / And answer, echoes, answer, dying, dying, dying," emerges most clearly at the end of the third strophe, with the echoed word *answer* helping to chime us back to the "Epithalamion" refrain. The poem, written some time between 1848 and 1850, performs two acts of revision. First, the "horns of Elfland," the voices of Spenserian and later romance tradition, "thinner, clearer, farther going," become identified with their own echoes. In the second stage, these natural echoes (Tennyson gave as an occasion for the poem a day on which he heard a bugle blown, at Killarney, with eight distinct echoes) are qualified for their mortality,

---

13. The most celebrated denial of "yet once more" in English poetry, the echoing tag of Poe's raven, "Nevermore," has far more significance than the self-deceiving account in the "The Philosophy of Composition" would indicate. The Romans heard the *caw, caw, caw* which we ascribe to the bird of omen as the prophetic *cras, cras, cras.* Poe's bird denies the promise of "tomorrow," by a suppressed or negative echo.

acoustical decay associated with human death. The turn in
the third strophe is toward another degree of metaphor. A
present trope of human, or allusive poetic rebound (in-
tertwined with an erotic relation between voices and presences) replaces the older romantic echoing which the poem
itself establishes as received tradition in its first twelve lines.
Of the bugle echoes, the poem declares:

> O love, they die in yon rich sky
>   They faint on hill or field or river:
> Our echoes roll from soul to soul,
>   And grow for ever and for ever.

The half-echoing formal device of the internal rhyme
throughout the poem now emerges, in the last line, in a full
repetition. Because of the whole context, it serves as far
more than iambic filler. The revised human ("our") echoes
point to a parable of poetic originality: the allusive echoings
rebounding from text to text themselves unroll a fable of
perpetuation, new versions of romantic summits, "old in
story," new in poem. Tennyson's echoes in this lyric are
matched, as is often the case in his descriptions of sound,
with pictorial figures. The effect of the whole is a transumption of the Wordsworthian and later imagery of reverberation. Emerson, in "The Poet," remarked of old metaphors,
"We are far from having exhausted the significance of the
few symbols we use. We can come to use them yet with a
terrible simplicity." The beautiful complexity figured in this
last phrase is that of revisionary, interpretive transumption.
In Tennyson's song, it has been applied to the image of
echoes itself.

It is out of what I believe was a deep response to the
metaleptic, summary resonance of Tennyson's lyric that
Benjamin Britten could make a setting of it that forms the
poetic centerpiece of his *Serenade,* Opus 31 for tenor, horn,
and strings (1943). This remarkable work has many inter-

pretive dimensions itself. Not the least of the impulses behind it were a personal love for the tenor, and a great ad-
miration for the skill of the horn player, for whom it was
composed. But the role of the horn, in particular, is most
complex: the emblematic *Waldhorn* of German romanticism, reclaimed for English, provides the accompanying,
echoing, interpreting voice for the array of English poetic
texts set in the *Serenade*. A night-piece itself, the whole
composition includes a witty, rather Marvellian passage
about the onset of evening by Charles Cotton; a tendentious
erotic reading of Blake's "The Sick Rose"; a purgatorial
setting of the anonymous sixteenth-century "Lyke-Wake
Dirge"; a cleansed, moonlight-rinsed hymn to Diana, the
"Queen and huntress, chaste and fair" from Ben Jonson's
Cynthia's Revels; and, finally, a rich, deep treatment of
Keats' sonnet "To Sleep." Night is itself mythopoetically
analyzed into phases or aspects by Britten's very choice of
poems. Enclosing them all within the framework of what is
essentially a Mahlerian genre—the group of song-texts for
solo voice and orchestra—works metaphorically also to re-
deem the sad, wanting history of English romantic music
by summing up over what should have been the tradition of
the English *Lied*. At a time of war with Germany, Britten
was taking romantic song back for Britain.

The setting of the Tennyson echo song occurs as the second movement of the sequence, between Cotton's archly set
catalogue of the slowing up of the day's activities and the
contextually powerful misreading of Blake's "dark, secret
love." Indeed, the "O love, they die in yon rich sky" line
from Tennyson is already conceived, in the setting, as a
lead-in to the more tortured aspects of night in the next
movement. In the Tennyson setting, the horn's memorable
and characteristic melody in descending thirds develops
from its echoing answer to elements in the vocal line. In the
setting of the final strophe, harmonic and rhythmic tension

increase to underline the erotic and personal resolution of Britten's reading of the turn to "our echoes." The actual presence of the horn in Britten's piece is, in the sense we have been exploring, an echo of (rather than an outright allusion to) its presence in, say, Weber. Its role vis-à-vis the strings and the vocal part, which alters in complex and significant ways from passage to passage, revises that of the piano as a textual interpreter, growing more complex from Schubert to Schumann to Hugo Wolf. But the sound of the horn in the setting of the song about echoes is not only canonical for the whole piece, but most clearly emblematic of its and the *Serenade's* transumptive poetic role. On which note of dying anecdotal fall, I conclude these remarks.

Appendix: The Trope of Transumption

I proposed exhuming, in my last chapter, the old rhetoricians' term *metalepsis* or *transumption* to name a figure of interpretive allusion. In view both of the rarity of the word and of its use for the figure corresponding to one of his revisionary relations between authorial psyches by Harold Bloom in his more recent writing, an examination of its confused but revealing history might be useful.

Among the very last of the tropes that effect change of meaning ("quae aliter significant"), according to Quintilian, is metalepsis or transumption. He describes it as providing a transition from one trope to another ("quae ex alio tropo in alium velut viam praestat"). It follows *catachresis* or *abusio* in his list, as it continues to do in Renaissance rhetorical handbooks. His discussion of it is not only dismissive ("rare and substandard"—"rarissimus et improbissimus") but puzzling, as we shall see shortly, as well. Transumption is rarely considered in modern taxonomies of metaphor. The *Rhetorica ad Herrenium,* so influential for later rhetorics, does not list it (although I believe that some of its functions are taken up by that treatise's trope of *permutatio* or *allegoria*). Neither does Cicero in *De oratore* (his discussions of wit in sections 54–71 of Book II apply much more to Renaissance poetic than do his discussions of tropes in Book III).

The Greek word *metalepsis* is from *metalambanô* (to partake in, succeed to, exchange, take in a new way, take in another sense [of words], and even to explain or understand—perhaps both of our modern meanings of "to take after" operate here). In patristic Greek, according to the lexicon of G. W. H. Lampe, the meanings include "partake," "participate," "suppose," "receive later or afterwards," "receive instead," "translate," "render," "transfer from literal to spiritual level," "refer type to antitype"—in short, to "interpret," as well as actively to involve the use of words in a different sense. Quintilian translated this word into Latin as *transumptio*. In English, the derived form *transumption* has meant, since the fifteenth century, variously a "copy or quotation"; "transfer or translation"; "transmutation or conversion." It has been identified with metaphor and, in logic, with the conversion of a hypothetical proposition into a categorical one—a movement from "If———then" to "But———therefore." All these meanings seem to generate what Leo Spitzer called a "semantic field," in this case, crowded with hermeneutical blossoms. We might return to "taking after," as it applies to understanding a prior meaning by pursuing and thereby emulating, as a kind of *summa* of all these.

But this is the name of a trope. In most descriptions of rhetorical figure, a kind of implicitly spatial language connects the representation with what it replaces—part for whole or vice versa, proximate or otherwise associated object or quality (even the animated synecdoche of I. A. Richards' tenor-vehicle distinction) and so forth. Save for dramatic irony, with its audience's—or reader's—proleptic sense of an outcome of which the dramatic speaker is unaware, and which engenders an interpretation more powerful than the raw intended meaning of the speaker himself, only transumption seems to involve a temporal sequence. Medieval and Renaissance rhetoricians, after some uncertainty, construe metalepsis as a trope of taking the consequent for the precedent (or sometimes, indeed, the other way), although Dante, as we shall see momentarily, is an exception. The consequence may be one of cause and effect, of a narrative pre- and post-—or, more generally, of a kind of allusive—connection.

Let us return to Quintilian's treatment of transumption (*Institutes* III. vi. 37–39). After some Greek examples, and some Latin ones modeled on them, he moves on to the nature of the metaleptic transition:

It is the nature of *metalepsis* to form a kind of intermediate step between the term transferred and the thing to which it is transferred, having no meaning in itself, but merely providing a transition. It is a *trope* with which to claim acquaintance, rather than one which we are ever likely to require to use. The commonest example is the following: *cano* is a synonym for *canto* and *canto* for *dico*, therefore *cano* is a synonym for *dico*, the intermediate step being provided by *canto*. We need not waste any more time over it.

(tr. H. E. Butler, Loeb Edition)

The relation of the Virgilian, high poetic term *cano* ("sing"—Homerically) to *canto* ("recite," "declaim," "repeat," "harp on," "speak a dramatic part," "incant") is governed by the phonemic and morphological similarity of the two words (there are, indeed, some near-puns in Quintilian's Greek examples as well). The passage from *canto* to *dico* involves more of a semantic twist, and in setting up the unstated subsequent phase—*dico* to *scribo*—it involves the major metaphor of *écriture* itself. We might translate the whole sequence into modern English by saying *sing* (for Milton or Pope or Wordsworth) means "say," which means "write," which means, for us today, "type," (with the operative pun that implies that typing is a type and thereby, an antitype, of writing). (Also, consider the transumptive chain: manuscript : handset type :: machine-set type : cold type).

We might observe that even in Quintilian's example there is an ambiguity. The trope of a trope is certainly to be described synchronically as a combination of figures, a trope connected to a trope, rather than merely leading to one. We might analyze such an example as Marlowe's "the

face that launched a thousand ships" as a synecdoche of
Helen operating on a metaphor of launching the ships as
causing the war (or even as an objectification of "Helen's
beauty" as "face," and the metaphor of the beauty doing the
"launching"). In any case, there is a transumption, or transition across, either Helen or her beauty. Samson's "dark
steps" (with its allusion to the Sophoclean "blind feet"—a
mere synecdoche for a blind man—in *Oedipus at Colonus*) or
the more famous Miltonic version of that figure, the celebrated "blind mouths" in *Lycidas*, might better be adduced.
In this latter case, a metaphoric *blind* operates on a synecdochic *mouths*, with a metalepsis across the unstated middle
term, *preachers*. It is as if the trope were alluding to its missing term. This is also a fortunate example, for it embodies a
diachronic dimension in its echo—and revision—of Sopho-
cles. But even for Quintilian—if we consider the Virgilian
and later poetic overtones of his particular textually relevant
example—there is a suppressed or implied diachrony as
well. Greek epic was *cantum*, literally "sung," and then later
written down; Latin poetry was written and then perhaps
recited as well as read, and it almost seems that in the example itself a case of historical replacement, or subsequent version, is present.

With the exception of an inclusion in a list of figures by
the third- to fourth-century A.D. Aristedes Quintilianus (he
mentions it along with epithet, metaphor, simile, synecdoche, periphrasis, allegory, and others as devices for *psucha-
gogia* or "mind-winning"), not much is made of metalepsis
until medieval rhetorics begin to expand on it through the
ingenious use of examples from Latin poetry. But ambiguity and confusion remain.

"For the rhetoricians," said St. Augustine, "metalepsis is
furthermore called a kind of dispute (*controversia*) which
sometimes called up blame, more often figurative paraphrase (*translationem*)." Isidore of Seville (*Etymologiarum*

VII, x), like Rabanus Maurus and Godefridus, calls it *irritans aut provocans* and adds another authority who interprets it as *dominans.* Certainly there remains from Quintilian on a nagging and irritating quality about this particular trope, even more unnecessary to a good rhetorical taxonomy than many others. There seem to be two branches of medieval rhetorical tradition that deal with the term. For one, it is a matter of *gradatio* or *climax,* covering situations that range from syntactic transitivity to a chain of actions embodied therein. An example is Virgil's line from the third eclogue, "torva leaena lupum sequitur, lupus ipse capellam" ("the grim lioness follows the wolf, the wolf himself the goat"— and, as the passage continues, "florentem cytisum sequitur lasciva capella, / te Corydon, o Alexi: trahit sua quemque voluptas" ("the lusty goat, the flowering clover, and Corydon, you, Alexis: each is drawn on by his pleasure"). Other such sequences range from the chain of damnation of original sin (thus Geoffroi de Vinseuf's *Poetria Nova:* "Hostis enim primus damnaverat Evam, Eva secunda virum, vir tertius omnes") to a somewhat less inexorably causal series, given by Matthew de Vendôme: "Ira movet litem, lis proelia, proelia mortem, mors lacrimas. . . ." (Wrath to strife to battle to death to tears). All of these examples seem to represent schemes, not tropes, and none requires interpretation.[1]

The main line of medieval and Renaissance exemplification of transumption descends through such writers as Isidore of Seville, Julian of Toledo, and the Venerable Bede. Isidore defines it (*Etymologia* I. xxxvii. 7) as a transition from a precedent to a subsequent, and gives a line from Persius' third satire—"Quaeve (Inque) manus cartae nodosaque venit arundo"—about taking in hand some paper and a knotty

---

1. Geoffroi de Vinseuf, *Poetria Nova,* 1147ff; Matthieu de Vendôme, *Ars Versificatoria,* III, 42. Texts and commentary in Edmond Faral, *Les arts poétiques du XIIe et du XIIIe siècle* (Paris, 1971).

reed-pen. We are to understand, he says, the "hand" as
"words" and the "pen" as "letters" ("Nam per manum verba,
per arundinem litterae significatae sunt"). Interestingly, this
is taken as a trope allusive of a traditional metonymy of *the
pen* for "writing." Julian is more elaborate. Aside from giving
Isidore's definition and example from Persius, he defines
metalepsis as "proceeding by degrees to that which is shown"
("dictio gradatim pergens ad id quod ostendit") and presents
as instances two Virgilian lines.

These remained the canonical examples up through the
eighteenth century. The first is from the *Aeneid* I, 60:

sed pater omnipotens speluncis abdidit atris
[hoc metuens]

([fearing this] the father omnipotent hid them in gloomy caverns)

Julian only cites this, but the traditional glossing may be
seen in the analysis by the sixteenth-century rhetorician
Susenbrotus (*Epitome tropam et schematum*), who argues that
"*gloomy* means *black*; *black*, *shadowy*; and *shadowy*, *deep*,"
with the implication that Jove imprisoned Aeolus' winds in
deep caverns.

Julian's other example is from the first eclogue:

Post aliquot mea regna videns mirabor aristas?

([after a long time] shall I, beholding what was my empire,
marvel at a few ears of grain?)

or, as it was traditionally misconstrued by Servius and
others, "Shall I wonder when I see my cottage, a domain
once mine, after many harvests?" Here the *post* seems to
apply to *aristas,* and thus requires the traditional interpretation: "For *ears* take *grain,* for *grain, years*" ("per aristas annos
ex fructibus computat: nam per aristas grana, per grana anni
significati sunt, pro eo quod singulis annis a terra collingun-

tur").[2] Or, again, as the humanist Susenbrotus gives it in a more crowded and belated glossing: "We take beards of grain for the ears themselves, ears for harvests, harvests for summers, and summers for years." ("Hic per aristas spicas, per spicas messes, per messes aestates, per aestates annons accipimus.")

Julian's contemporary, Bede, with Christian *pudeur* suppresses all classical examples, and gives instead a verse from Psalms (128:2), "Labores fructuum tuorum manducabis"— or, in the King James version, "For thou shalt eat the labour of thine hands" (and glosses it: "Labores' enim posuit pro his quae laborando adquiruntur bonis").

Dante, in his letter (ca. 1319) to Can Grande about the structure of the whole *Commedia,* provides a rhetorical taxonomy of what he calls the form or method of treatment (*modus tractandi,* as opposed to *modus tractatus* or form of the text). He calls this form or mode "poetic, fictive, descriptive, digressive, transumptive" [with the last term seeming to sum up the others] and at the same time proceeding by "definition, division, proof, refutation and positing examples" ("peoticus, fictivus, descriptivus, digressivus, transumptivus, et cum hoc diffinitivus, divisivus, probativus, improvativus et exemplorum positivus.") The latter five terms are logical as well as rhetorical, but the first are poetic. E. R. Curtius adduces Alexander of Hales' distinction between the *historicus vel transumptivus* ("historical or figurative") modes of representation employed by poetry, and assumes that transumptive means metaphorical in some general way. (One might also cite the commentary on Mussato's *Ecerinide,* which, in making *transumptio* a trope of personification or animation of the inanimate—"ex eo quod id quod est animal, attributur ad non animal"—puts it into a traditional realm of metaphor.)

2. Julian of Toledo, *De Tropis,* in Henricus Kiel, *Grammatici Latini* (Leipzig, 1857–80), V, 324.

Later medieval rhetorics generally try to accommodate three principles, usually by glossing the traditional Virgilian examples:

(1) There is a transition from one trope to another;

(2) The tropes in question are in some way anterior and posterior;

(3) There will be one or more unstated, but associated or understood figures, transumed by the trope, but which are to be reconstructed by interpretation.

In any case, the trope of metalepsis is an allusive one (as well as being elusive), whether we consider the subsequent as alluding to the precedent or to the intervening series. The near *paranomasias* in Quintilian's discussion seem to return from time to time in later commentaries—so Richard Sherry, in his *A Treatise of Schemes and Tropes* (London, 1550), telling us that "transsupcion is when by degrees we go to that is shewed as: he hyd hym selfe in the black dennes," comments, "By blacke is understande ful of darkenes and consequently stepe down and very depe." (The *steep/deep* rhyme comes purely from the poetics of his own glossing.)

Erasmus likens transumption to catachresis or *abusio*, the last instances of which are closer to what Cicero calls *collatio*, in which a simile and a metaphor are combined. I quote the excellent translation of *De Copia* (1514) by D. B. King and H. D. Rix: "Similar to *abusio* is *metalepsis*, called *transumptio* by the Latins. This is when we proceed by steps to that which we wish to express, as: he hid in dark caves. For the connotation is of black caves, from black obscure, and from this finally, extreme depth. Thus the Greeks call sharp what they wish to be thought swift. But a use for this figure occurs more often in verse than in prose, and it can be considered a type of synecdoche just as those which follow" (Book I, Chapter XXI).

Henry Peacham, in *The Garden of Eloquence,* follows Erasmus, Sherry, and other commentators: "Metalepsis, when we goe by degrees to that which is shewed, a fygure seldom used of Oratours, and not ofte of Poets, as to saye, he lyeth in a darcke Dungeon. Now in speaking of darcknesse, we understand closenesse, by closenesse, blacknesse, by blacknesse, deepnesse. *Virgil* by eares of Corn, he signifyeth harvestes, by harvestes, sommers, and by sommers, yeares." The English version of the Latin gloss raises the question of like sound: the transumption might be said to be of *ears* for *years.* A French *symboliste* or an English or American modernist poet might employ just such a trope by writing "years of corn." Certainly we get this device in wit and jokes all the time (but see Cicero, *De Oratore* II, 263: "gravium autem et iocorum unam esse rationem," which both Renaissance poetic and Freud understood well). The older rhetorics might associate this with catachresis, or abusio, a wrenching of sense hovering between the brilliant and the disreputable.

It should only be noted here that this substitution of a like-sounding word for an expected one is quite important in modern poetry, although it is usually considered as an aspect of the unconscious, freely-associative, "automatic," or dreamlike apparatus of symbolist and even surrealist theory. Consider, for example, Wallace Stevens' "Like the clashed edges of two words that kill" (from "Le Monocle de Mon Oncle"): here the transumption is of the missing term *swords,* the word *words* being a sort of synecdochic part of the longer *swords.* Or Hart Crane's "high in the azure steeps" (for *deeps*) in "At Melville's Tomb"; or Tennyson, in "A Dream of Fair Women": "Yearnings that can never be exprest / By signs or groans or tears" (for *sighs*); or John Ashbery's memory of "the mooring of starting out, that day so long ago," where *mooring* is substituted for the expected word *morning,* a particular time being able to function as a fixed point for extravagant memory. But neither of these examples constitutes punning. Each is more like an allusive half-echo, making "a change from one trope to another."

"But the sence is much altered and the hearers conceit strangely entangled by the figure *Metalepsis,* which I call the farfet, as when we had rather fetch a word a great way off then to use one nerer hand to expresse the matter aswel and plainer," remarks George Puttenham in what may be the most elaborate account of the trope in English (*The Arte of English Poesie, 1596*). He continues:

And it seemeth the deviser of this figure, had a desire to please women rather then men: for we use to say by manner of Proverbe: things farrefet and deare bought are good for Ladies: so in this manner of speach we use it, leaping over the heads of a great many words, we take one thing that is furdest off, to utter our matter by: as *Medea* cursing her first acquaintance with prince Jason, who had very unkindly forsaken her, said:

> *Woe worth the mountaine that the maste bare*
> *Which was the first causer of all my care.*

Where she might as well have said, woe worth our first meeting, or woe worth the time that *Jason* arrived with his ship at my fathers cittie in *Colchos,* when he tooke me away with him, and not so farre off as to curse the mountaine that bare the pinetree, that made the mast, that bare the sailes, that the ship sailed with, which caried her away. . . . Virgill said:

> *Post multas mea regna videns mirabor aristas.*

Thus in English.

> *And after manny a stubble shall I come*
> *And wonder at the sight of my kingdome.*

By stubble the Poet understoode yeares, for harvests come but once every yeare, at least ways with us in Europe. This is spoken by the figure of farre-fet.   (III, 18)

For Puttenham, transumption is not so much a sort of Clevelandism, despite his name for it, as a device of severe

compression, and hence, of wit. His example concerning
Medea's cursing the mountain is a metaleptic causal chain,
like that of some of the medieval theorists. More amusing is
his further misprision of Virgil for whose "*Post aliquot. . . .*"
he substitutes a `*multas* to give the line a self-contained poi-
gnancy of complaint. But he misses the opportunity to
work through the whole chain of *ears–harvests–summers–
years.* In any event, though the trope is an occasion for his
own joking, we may observe that metalepsis fetches signification from afar in time as well as in semiotic space—
that the far-fetcher is an after-taker as well.

An amusing musical analogy occurs in Joachim Burmeister's *Musica Poetica* (1606), an attempt to apply rhetorical
concepts, including tropes and schemes, to the analysis of
High Renaissance polyphonic music. The system is itself a
trope of rhetorical figures, putting music for language. Burmeister assigns certain traditional figures to the realm of
harmony, and others to melody; among the former, he lists,
just after "fugue proper" (*fuga realis*), metalepsis, which he
defines as "that manner of fugue in which two melodies are
transumed from here to there in Harmony and converted
into fugue" ("Metalepsis . . . est talis habitus Fugae, in duo
Melodiae in Harmonia hinc inde transsumuntur et in fugam
vertuntur"). But he goes on to add to this puzzling formulation that the most splendid example of this (*exemplum lucu-
lentissum*) is a motet by Orlando di Lasso, "De ore prudentis". If we look at the opening measures of the five-part
piece in question, a clear, if reductive, version of a transumptive scheme, rather than trope, emerges.

For the soprano and alto start out, in usual canonic imitation, with the whole first line: "De ore prudentis procedit
mel" ("from the mouth of the wise honey comes forth").
But the entrance of the second tenor and bass parts, in the
fifth and sixth measures, is on the phrase "procedit mel"
only. The "procedit mel" setting itself literally "comes

forth" from the two-part texture already being sung (the fifth part, the first tenor, enters last, with the full line of text, in imitation of the first two voices). In the second tenor and bass the initial phrase, "De ore prudentis," then, is taken to be transumed.

The hearer, in other words, must infer or understand it from its subsequent words (the predicate), which enter in fugal imitation not of the opening melodic phrase, but of the following one. This is a good structural, or schematic, instance of metalepsis as omission of one or more intermediate or preceding terms, and certainly as "ab eo quod praecedit id quod sequitur insinuans," in the words of Bede quoted earlier. It might also be added that, given the melodic flourish called a *melisma* on the word *mel*—a conventional bit of sixteenth-century musical "word-painting"—the relation of text to setting might have been sufficiently forceful to Burmeister as to allow him to see the metaleptic fugal scheme itself as a higher order of emblematic representation of the meaning of the text: from the mouth of the opening "voices" of the fugue proceeds the honey of the later entrances, and the hermeneutic of musical structure depends upon metalepses all the time. (This is perhaps why polyphonic structure is so fundamentally echoic in itself as to vitiate the force of the analogy when applied to certain kinds of music.)

Giambattista Vico, in discussing the development of metaphor in human history, propounds a wonderful series of natural fables of his own to explain the sources of personification and synecdoche in phenomenology and social use. Transumption is not a trope for him (his master figures, like Kenneth Burke's, are metaphor, metonymy, synecdoche, and irony). But consider the following observation (from *The New Science* II. 2. iii. 407):

That bit of synecdoche and metonymy, *Tertia messis erat* ("It was the third harvest"), was doubtless born of a natural necessity, for it took more than a thousand years for the astronomical term "year" to arise among the nations; and even now the Florentine peasantry say, "We have reaped so many times," when they mean "so many years." And that knot of two synecdoches and a metonymy, *Post aliquot, mea regna videns, mirabor, aristas?* ("After a few harvests shall I wonder at seeing my kingdoms?"), betrays only too well the poverty of expression of the first rustic times, in which the phrase "so many ears of wheat"—even more particular than harvests— was used for "so many years." And because of the excessive poverty of the expression, the grammarians have assumed an excess of art behind it.[3]

If this is not a severe deconstruction of classical and Renaissance rhetoric, it is in any event a tough and sly end run around it: Vico knows that the line he quotes—and calls "a knot of two synecdoches and a metonymy"—is the traditional example of transumption. But again, like the others, he misconstrues Virgil's line in the traditional way.

In another passage (II. 2. vi. 482), Vico discusses "the usage which has come down in the languages of many Christian nations of taking heaven for God." (One might wonder whether this trope is in fact a metonymy? a synecdoche? a metaphor? or—as Kafka might have put it—an unwitting and therefore dramatic irony?) He treats of Italian and Spanish examples, and then considers the *"sacrebleu"* euphemism in French (which is obviously a kind of circumlocution such as is contrived by British rhyming slang):

The French say *bleu* for blue, and since blue is a form of sense-perception, they must have meant by *bleu* the sky; and just as the gentile nations used "sky" for Jove, the French must have used *bleu* for God in that impious oath of theirs, *moure bleu!*, "God's death!"; and they still say *parbleu!* "by God!"

This assumption of etymological causation is itself a mytho-poetic conceit; we might take the argument from rhyming

3. Giambattista Vico, *The New Science,* trans. Thomas G. Bergin and Max Harold Fisch (rev. ed., Ithaca, 1970), 89–90.

slang and say that the *bleu* for *dieu* was perfectly transumptive—*bleu : cieux : Dieu,* like *ears : harvests : : summers : years* in
the earlier example.

A few other rhetoricians who list the trope are:

Minturno, *De poeta* (Venice, 1559) VI, MMMiii. *Metalepsis* comes
between *abusio* and *ironia:* "Commutantur quoque vocabula cum
pro adultero sumitur Paris, pro callido Ulysses, pro invicto
Achilles. Et nunc Paris cum semiviro comitatu. Videlicet Aeneam
uti effeminatum, mollemque intelligit." (He then gives the ears of
corn and dark cave examples.)

Bartolomeo Cavalcanti, *La retorica* (Ferrara, 1559) Y6$_v$: He glosses
the traditional dark caves, not quoting the Virgilian line, but only
citing the phrase as an example: ". . . come, se alcuno parlando
d'una profondissima balza, la chiamasse nera; per la qual parola
intenderemo prima oscura, e per mezzo di questa passeremo
all'inteso significato di profunda. È certamente [he adds] questo
modo molto improprio. . . ."

Joanne Susenbroto, *Epitome tropum ac schematum* (London, 1562),
A7$_v$–A8: Quoted above.

Petrus Mosellanus, *Tabulae de schematibus et tropis* (Deventer,
1527), B3: He adds to his only example (the cave) the observation:
"Verum huius tropi usus magis incidet in carmine, quam in ora-
tione soluta."

Thomas Wilson, *The Arte of Rhetorique* (London, 1553, 1560):
"Transumption is, when by degrees wee go to that which is to be
shewed. As thus: Such a one lieth in a dark Dungeon: now, in
speaking of darknesse, we understand closenesse, by closenesse,
we gather blacknesse, and by blacknesse, we judge deepnesse."
The Virgilian line has vanished totally. Compare this with Richard
Sherry's treatment a few years earlier.

Thomas Farnaby, *Index rhetoricus* (London, 1625): "Transcendit
medijs Metalepsis ad altum: Hinci movet Euphrates bellum. Mirabor aristas."

John Smith, *The Mysterie of Rhetorique* (London, 1657): He makes a remarkable departure, saying that metalepsis operates "when divers Tropes are shut up in one word: as 2 Kings 2:9. I pray thee let me have a double portion of thy spirit."

Vossius, *Commentariorum rhetoricum* (1605) II, 162: "Metalepsis vocatur tum quando ex antecedente intelligentur consequens aut ex consequente antecedens."

C. C. Dumarsais, *Traité des tropes* (1730): He discusses the trope at some length, as a type of metonymy, mostly giving the consequent for the antecedent, and vice versa, with both Latin and French examples.

Pierre Fontanier, *Les Figures du discours* (1821–30): In this elaborate work, he places *métalepse* between *allusion* and *association* among his "figures d'expression par réflexion," and explores a variety of devices of indirection in his examples, including displacement, command given for report, etc. Fontanier's treatise has been widely discussed by contemporary theorists, including Gérard Genette and Paul Ricoeur.

The whole Renaissance is in a sense a transumption of antique culture, and the very concept of being reborn (*gennethê anôthen,* in the words of Jesus to Nicodemus, John 3:3–8) is a partial misconstruction of the Greek. It gives "born again" instead of "born from above"—born from wind and water instead of from the unmentioned earth of the old Adam and the old birth. Rebirth is a revision of original birth. This process of taking hold of something poetically in order to revise it upward, as it were, canceling and transforming (Hegel seems to use *Aufhebung* in such a constellation of ways) is a metaleptic act in the broadest sense. It is taking after—in the sense of "pursuing"—what one has been fated to take after as a resembling descendant. Renaissance poetic thought is full of such prehensions and apprehensions. It blossoms with revisions of revisions. These can be schematized in radical Protestant theology— Luther revises Paul's revision of the Hebrew sect still based on the Law, and Milton and Bunyan revise Luther's revision. Or they can be manifested in the revision of poetic genres—pastoral from Virgil to Mantuan to *The Shepheardes Calender* to Book VI of *The Faerie Queene* to *Lycidas* to Marvell's mower poems, for example. They can even be implicit in systems of interpretation—mythographic and biblical exegesis, for instance, when combined and reinterpreted in the great poetic machinery of *The Faerie Queene* or *Paradise Lost*.

Michael Drayton, a splendid poet and attentive Spenserian, glosses the river Meander in Lycia, in one of his *Heroic Epistles* ("Rosalind to Henry II") by allusion to its proverbially twisting course, and adds: "Hereupon are intricate turnings by a transumptive and Metonymicall kind of speech called Meanders." Not only do we have a prior allusion as part of a trope, but one of those self-descriptive images that point to the nature of their own language: *meandering,* as a figure, is an "intricate turning" of a river of sense going back on itself recursively. (The "natural" emblem of flowing water as eloquence is lurking here; Dr. Johnson sensed, but did not explicitly grasp, this in Sir John Denham's famous and influential couplet about Thames and Themes—Johnson condemned it for merely manifesting what was there originally.) The theme of a river going back on itself, widely imitated from Ovid's *Heroïdes* as well as from scripture, gets to be associated with the theme of heroic complaint. Perhaps for Drayton it was associated with the allusiveness, as well as the rhetorical turning, of a genre so well established even in Chaucer's time.

Not only particularly preexistent metaphors, but formal structures—and M. H. Abrams and, more recently, Paul Fry, have shown us authoritatively the intricate turnings of the transumption of a previously public form in the history of the ode[4]—are recreated metaleptically. So are genres. Classical rhetoric was a system for enforcing direct persuasion by force of words. The Renaissance interpreted this figuratively as psychogogic for poetic truth. All taxonomies of rhetorical figure have in fact been themselves interpretive. The history of the particular concepts of metaphor, synecdoche, metonymy, and irony—not to speak of notions like allegory, parable, fable, fiction, figure, image, and type—is itself a meandering one. The fate of "transumption" is more than usually tangled as well. But I hope that its turnings may be seen to be curious knots in a panchronic garden, even as they move in and out of bosks and groves of local error.

4. M. H. Abrams, "Structure and Style in the Greater Romantic Lyric," in *From Sensibility to Romanticism,* ed. Frederick W. Hilles and Harold Bloom (New York, 1965), 527–60. Paul H. Fry, *The Poet's Calling in the English Ode* (New Haven, 1980).

Index of Authors Cited